T0209578

STRENGTH
on the Water

MELISSA J DELLACA

WESTBOW
PRESS®
A DIVISION OF THOMAS NELSON
& ZONDERVAN

WestBow Press books may be ordered through booksellers or by contacting:

WestBow Press
A Division of Thomas Nelson & Zondervan
1663 Liberty Drive
Bloomington, IN 47403
www.westbowpress.com
844-714-3454

ISBN: 978-1-6642-6485-4 (sc)
ISBN: 978-1-6642-6486-1 (hc)
ISBN: 978-1-6642-6487-8 (e)

Library of Congress Control Number: 2022907714

Print information available on the last page.

WestBow Press rev. date: 5/5/2022

CONTENTS

CHAPTER 1
Reclaimed

The cursor blinked steadily on the screen. A blank, outlined box stared back at me. What words could I type to fill this space that would encompass the directive: "Tell us a little about yourself"?

Divorced. Single mother. College student. Lonely. Exhausted.

Somehow, I didn't think these words were going to help me out in this particular task. What did they want to hear?

Active! Ambitious! Spontaneous!

I shut the laptop as my bedroom door opened.

"Mohhhmm," my son said, dragging the title out in a long, whiny slur.

"What's up, buddy? What do you need?"

Jacob climbed up on my lap as I sat at my desk. The pretty glass desk next to the posh cream leather office chair I was sitting on. The one his dad had bought me not long before he moved out.

"I'm thirsty," he whimpered.

"Dude, you've had too many drinks already. I don't think it's a good idea to have any more. How about I come lay next to you for a few minutes, okay?"

We walked across the family room and down the short hallway to his bedroom. His brother was in the top bunk.

"I'm never going to fall asleep!" Michael burst out upon our arrival. "Jake won't shut up and I have to get up early to work out with Dad. I'm never going to get enough sleep!"

"I'm sorry, I know," I attempted to placate him. "Give him a few more minutes and he'll settle down."

"Yeah, right." Michael sighed but didn't argue anymore.

I slid into bed beside Jake, who'd already climbed up and was smack dab in the middle of the bed.

"Scootch over, buddy. I'm going to fall off the bed."

I pushed Jake over and tucked his favorite stuffed dog under his arm. Then I draped my arm over his little body and nestled my head above his, inhaling the smell of recently washed hair. I couldn't complain too much. I loved laying here next to him and snuggling my baby, just as I'd enjoyed my older two when they were this age. But I knew I couldn't afford to fall asleep here with so much left to get done tonight.

This was my productive time, when the kids were all in bed and I could get some homework or studying done. Maybe that's not what I *had* been doing, but I would get to it when they were asleep, and I could concentrate. I'd briefly been distracted by this dating website; I'd been trying to figure out which one was the best. There were too many! And now dating *apps*—lots of those too. Knowing which would yield the right guy was the real question. Farmers Only? Probably not my type. Tinder? Hookups. I was hoping this newest site would find the dashing yet responsible Prince Charming who was out there just waiting to be discovered.

After several minutes, Jake's breathing became more regular, and I slowly extracted myself from under his comforter. Michael didn't say anything as I crept across the room to the doorway. I quietly closed the door and walked down the short hallway, but as I passed Olivia's room, I heard her singing softly. I paused and leaned in to better hear what she was singing. I couldn't make it out, but it made me happy to hear her sweet voice. She was probably making up a song, as she often did. She seemed to work out her feelings this way.

I padded across the tiled floor. The fuzzy socks I wore protected me from the cold tiles and dulled the sound of my footsteps. I walked into my bedroom, surveying the updated surroundings. The desk in the corner was still new enough to my eyes, and the long wall opposite the windows appeared bare without the long, low dresser. The tall dresser was now turned diagonally in the corner with a small TV on top, taking up more space and making the area feel less empty. The new feminine duvet cover claimed the bed as mine, no longer belonging to anyone else. My things were spread out between both nightstands—all mine as well.

Walking over to the desk, I unzipped the backpack and pulled out a binder to see what was on the docket for the evening. I reviewed the weekly planner inside and remembered the assignment I needed to finish and upload tonight for Histology and Embryology. Then there was the test in Head and Neck Anatomy tomorrow. I would need to review the flashcards I had created. Once again, I silently cursed these classes I had to take. Would I ever use all the information I was required to learn? As fascinating as it was, once I passed all my boards and was a Registered Dental Hygienist (RDH), would I really be pulling out facts on embryology or neck anatomy to help my patients?

My attention drifted to the laptop. It sprung to life as I opened it, the picture of Navajo Lake appearing with Jake and Olivia splashing in the water and Michael close behind in the kayak. That had been a good trip. I'd felt so accomplished using my new hitch on the minivan to tow our camp trailer up the steep, curving roads to the lake. We'd rarely been on fun outings like this, and I was determined to show the kids all the great places right in our backyard. I suppose I also wanted to demonstrate that I could do the things I wanted to all by myself, without a man.

I typed in my password, and the blank gray box was staring back at me again. I opened another tab and brought up Facebook. I hadn't posted anything since the separation and divorce that explained my situation and had only joined social media quite recently to connect with friends and family, a connection I needed right now. Some faraway friends that weren't in my daily life had noticed that I only had pictures of the kids and myself and had started sending me private messages asking questions. I told them the truth but didn't want to get caught up in negativity, so I hadn't posted anything about it. Suddenly I decided it was time. "Homework or Dating Site?" I posted, then immediately clicked on the other browser tab, not waiting for any commentary. Back to the gray box.

> I'm a pretty well-rounded gal. I need to get out and do things! I'm the kind of girl who likes to get muddy but also get dressed up for a night on the town. I love music of all sorts—playing, singing, listening to it, dancing to it. Currently attending dental hygiene school. An adventurer at heart, I have been enjoying new things on my own and with my three kids (ages fourteen, ten and six). I recently took up triathlon training and have participated in a few this last year. If it involves water, the answer is yes!

I pressed submit, and the website took me back to the homepage. Having completed the required information, I would now be allowed to peruse the goods. No swipe right or left on this medium, but I could scroll down through pictures with ages attached. James, age thirty-five. Steve, age forty-four. Ryan, age thirty-one. I squirmed internally at the last one. Thirty-one, really? Wasn't this too young for me? I'd set the parameter at "ages 31-49" to give me a wide range of options, but I doubted I could feel comfortable with a man four years younger than me. Somehow, fifteen years older seemed more acceptable. I clicked on his picture, curious now. He was cute, but I was hoping to find something that validated my concern. As I read through his bio, my smugness leaked out. Never married, no kids, how could he ever understand my world?

Just then, a sound came from the computer. A collapsed chat box in the lower right of the screen started flashing with the number one in red—one new chat. A message already? I was nervous and excited at the same time, wondering if I should wait a few minutes so as not to appear too eager. My hands were a little shaky, and my heart beat faster. I took a deep breath, my eyes not leaving the flashing red number one. I clicked on it.

"Hey, what are you up to?" The message identified the sender as Ryan, age thirty-one. It was almost as if he had been listening to my dismissal and was challenging me.

"Procrastinating studying. How about you?" Send. I watched, my heart pumping as I waited for his response.

"Oh, hanging out. Why not procrastinate some more? You're pretty hot by the way."

Whoosh. The adrenaline rush surged through my body. He thought I was hot? How was I supposed to answer that? I mentally swept through the pictures I'd used for my profile—a couple of random selfies, a triumphant post-triathlon pic, a photo of myself dressed up for an event. Which one did he like best? Okay, back to the issue at hand; how should I respond?

"Haha, thanks! You're not bad yourself. ;) So, what does hanging out mean exactly?" Send.

It was impressive how quickly flirting had come back after all the years of being married. I wasn't sure I would remember how to do it and I'd worried that I would feel weird about it. Nope, it felt natural and not weird at all. After years of an empty marriage, I was more than ready to get on with it.

"Oh, you know, just watching Netflix. Chatting with hot babes, lol. I see you like adventures."

"Nice *Napoleon Dynamite* reference," I typed. "I try to be adventurous. What do you do around here for fun?"

In the smallish desert town, there wasn't much of a nightlife, but there were lots of places to explore nearby. I wondered if he was an outdoor adventurer or if this conversation was about to turn where too many often did. Lots of guys were looking for more of an indoor adventure, so to speak.

"Well, it involves water..." The dot, dot, dot meant he was waiting for me to fill in the blank.

"Then the answer is yes! Haha," I responded.

"Have you ever been skimboarding?"

"Not yet! But my friends take their kids down to the river, and it sounds fun. You must be a pro."

"Something like that," he typed back. "Saturday?" he proposed.

"Sounds great!"

Luckily, my kids would be at their dad's for the weekend, so I knew I was available. Some women may have been surprised at such a quick invitation, but this is exactly what I liked. I had wasted too much time with back-and-forth chat sessions. I would start to really like a guy, then I'd meet him and realize it would never work out. It was better to connect quickly and move on if it was a no-go.

This *was* an unusual first date for me though, but honestly that boded well. He was creative and fun! Most of my first dates were quick meets for frozen yogurt since I didn't drink coffee. It worked well because if it was obviously not going to happen, it was over in an hour or less. If we clicked, then we could always extend to dinner or something else. Skimboarding would be a bit of a risk, but hey, either way it'd be fun! I wasn't afraid for a guy to see me in my bathing suit on a first date. I grew up on swimming teams and boating with my family, so I wasn't kidding that I would say yes if it involved water. We set a time and meeting place and said our goodnights after a little more flirtation. I really did need to get that homework done.

When I was prepared for tomorrow and my eyes were struggling to stay open, I climbed into bed. Sprawling sideways, I took up the entire queen-size mattress. The first few weeks after my ex-husband had moved out, I'd stayed on my side, rarely even disturbing "his side" of the bed. Then one night I had decided I was done with that.

STRENGTH ON THE WATER

I'd gotten into bed from the opposite side that I normally did and stretched out, intentionally filling up as much space as I could. It had stuck. I checked and double-checked my alarm as usual. It was set for 4:40 a.m. and I counted the hours on my fingers. It was 11:25 p.m., so basically 11:30, 12:30, 1:30—I would get about five hours of sleep. I had wasted a lot of time on the chat with Skimboarder, 31. Worth it.

CHAPTER 2
No Excuses

The alarm sounded from my cell phone. I sat straight up and paused a moment to calm my breath before shutting off the alarm and heading across the room. My cycling clothes were laid across the countertop ready for me. I quickly used the bathroom, got dressed, and within ten minutes I was at the meeting point.

Three were already there waiting as I unloaded my bike from the minivan, and two more arrived as I was strapping on my helmet and pulling on my gloves. We would ride a pre-determined loop, usually around forty-five minutes, then finish with either a run or a swim. Today was a run. It wasn't my strength, but it was getting better. I had pushed through my mental block last year and worked up to a half marathon. Even so, I didn't love it. There wasn't much discussion due to the cold. Beeps emanated from the watches and phones surrounding me as we all started our fitness trackers, and we were off.

Although riding in the cold wasn't my favorite, I liked being out in the dark. The world remained asleep. There wasn't much movement outside besides our draft line. Six lights shining forward with flashing tail-lights behind. I loved how it felt to empty my mind of worries and focus on the road. Just settling in and doing the work. There was only the bike in front of me, the push and pull of my feet clipped into the pedals, and the burn in my quads. When we made it back to our starting point and unclipped it was still dark. We switched out our shoes, some making the quick change into jogging shorts. Then following Stephanie's lead, we made our way to the trail.

Stephanie was the leader of the pack, this small band of triathletes. They'd branded themselves the "No Excuses" group. I had met them by chance one morning the year before, a moment I'd always be grateful for. They had finished a triathlon just days before and were hanging out in the hot tub at the gym. I had completed a swim in the outdoor pool and decided to hop in the hot tub to enjoy the sunrise. They quickly struck up conversation, complimenting me on my swim—they had been watching. I was a swimmer and had been thinking about getting into triathlon earnestly the past year. They invited me to join them for their next swim. The rest, as they say, was history.

It was exactly what I'd needed at the time. When I met them, my husband Ezra had been gone for a couple of months. He'd been distant, which wasn't new, but things had gotten even worse. Ezra had begun leaving often in the evenings or on the weekends to do things on his own, saying he needed time to think or decompress. He would always make it home for dinner with the kids, then some nights he'd leave again to finish up work or go to the gym. Something was off, but I couldn't put my finger on it. Then one night when I'd asked him if anything was wrong, he blurted out that he was unhappy and wanted a divorce. I had collapsed to my knees and sobbed, devastated. He'd expressed discontent about certain things before, like how I kept the house or something, but this was unexpected.

We had gone to counseling after that, but he'd never seemed to follow through with anything the counselor challenged us to do at home. His actions had demonstrated that he wasn't interested in nurturing our relationship. Naturally, I had suspicions of another woman, but Ezra had denied it repeatedly. I think he'd decided he was done with me for quite some time, and I was upset that he wouldn't have confided in me. After months, I'd asked him to move out if he didn't want to be with me or show that he was willing to invest in us. It hurt too much to try so hard and feel rejected again and again. Surprisingly, he hadn't put up much of a fight. In fact, he'd already leased an apartment.

After Ezra moved out I had too much time on my hands. Not necessarily when the kids were around, but when they were gone it was like my world was falling apart. *How did I end up here? What did I do wrong? This isn't the life I planned!* I had realized quickly that I needed something to fill my time when they were away. The first weekend hadn't been a big deal, in fact it was revitalizing to take some naps and organize the house.

But the next weekend was a different story. I'd gone to Home Depot to get a curtain rod for the sliding door that led from the kitchen to the small deck. I didn't like that everyone could see inside our house, but Ezra had never wanted to hang anything. No nails in the walls. Not for paintings, curtain rods, *nada*. Well, it was my house now, and I was determined to make it feel that way. After I'd selected the perfect dark iron rod and fit it into the back of the van, I climbed in the driver side and went to start the engine. I couldn't do it. I couldn't go home. No one was there, it was dark, and I would be all alone and sad. My breathing escalated and I began to cry uncontrollably. I was having a panic attack.

This had only happened once before—in my closet, on the day I finally called my parents to tell them what was going on. I had really tried to keep it a secret. If Ezra and I could work things out, they'd never have to know. But that night in my closet I couldn't breathe, I couldn't think, and all I knew was that I needed someone. So, I had called my parents. I'd heard the concern and fear in their voices, but the words wouldn't come out. When I had been able to vocalize that I was okay, it was a start. But they still had no idea what was wrong. They'd started making guesses, hoping I could at least confirm or deny. Bit by bit, I'd gotten it out and they talked me through it.

In the minivan at Home Depot, I hadn't wanted to call my parents. I had needed someone who could come in the flesh to help me, and my parents were hours away. Instead, I had called a friend who happened to be on a date with her husband at the time. She met me at Home Depot, sat in the passenger seat, and talked me down until I knew I would be able to drive home. Once I had come to my senses, I was horrified that I'd interrupted her time with her husband. But she was incredibly kind and loving and had made sure I knew how important I was to her.

This is why I was grateful for this group. They filled my time, gave me things to look forward to, and exhausted me physically which was helpful in its own way. Under their direction I had learned the ropes of riding in a group including signaling, drafting, and how to shift through gears more efficiently. Stephanie's sister Chloe was also part of the group, and their dad brought experience and patience. On my first ride, he had helped me remove all the non-essential reflectors and such off my bike. I had gotten the picture that having these marked me as a newbie and was embarrassing. This family had pulled in individuals one-by-one to their way of life. Stephanie made the schedule, and you could plan on 5:00 a.m. Monday through Friday with some combination of bike, run, or pool swim. Long rides, trail runs, or open water swims were usually reserved for Saturdays.

As we started slowly jogging, the trail wound down along the river. We swatted away a cloud of gnats. This is when the talking would start—the gossip, the chit-chat. I was the only one of this crew that had been divorced. They still seemed eager to hear more of my story and the ongoing juicy details.

"Did you get on that new dating website yet?" Chloe asked.

"About that…I did, and I already have a date for Saturday!"

Heads whipped over to me with big eyes.

"Tell us! What does he look like? Do you have a picture?" Jenny rapid fired questions. Jenny was an adorable, petite blonde who had especially been living through me as of late. She wasn't very happy in her marriage and seemed to be checking out the prospect of living life on the other side.

"I'll show you when we finish. He's actually super cute, but maybe a little young for me."

I got some woo-woos and whistles for that. Everett, who was hanging back, moved forward hearing the commotion.

"What's this? Too young? Whatever, go for it. You deserve it!"

Here was another reason I liked hanging out with these guys. They pushed me past my comfort zone physically, and emotionally they were supporting me and helping my confidence as well.

"I don't know if he can handle my kids," I protested.

"Who cares!" Jenny piped in. "He's young and hot and wants to take you out. Have a good time, it's not like you have to marry the guy."

Fair point and one I had considered myself. I had already dated a few guys that weren't exactly marriage material. Sometimes I just needed companionship, especially when my kids were with their dad. The conversation tapered down as we finished the run.

Jenny hadn't forgotten about his picture and prodded me when we got back to the cars. She ogled his profile picture for a while before she slowly gave me back my phone.

"Enjoy Saturday for me, Mel," she said with a wink.

I laughed and climbed into my minivan. I always liked when people called me Mel. Short for Melissa, I liked the familiarity of it. Jenny was one of those sweet girls that called me Mel the first day we met. I always envied women like that. I guess I was too formal, or at least a little more reserved.

Time to get home and wake up the kids. Michael was back from the gym, dressed for school, and eating breakfast at the table. Speaking of shortening names, we never called him Mike. If anyone did that, he would correct them. He was Michael. He was wearing one of his polos and a pair of jeans—his own personal uniform. He could wear whatever he liked at his school, but I'm pretty sure he'd picked this up from his dad who wore polos every day to work.

It could be difficult to find clothes that worked for Michael as he was very slender but also quite tall at the same time. Getting pants to fit his waist and not appear as if he were escaping a flood was tricky. Michael was also analytical like his dad. He was extremely intelligent, and school came easily to him.

"How did you sleep?" I asked him.

"Fine, once Jake went to sleep," he responded.

I didn't have to ask him if he had his assignments done or if he was prepared for his tests. I never worried about these things with Michael or Olivia, they were both incredibly responsible.

"So, I have clinic till five. I think it's Olivia's dinner night." I checked the menu on the fridge. Yep, Michael was off the hook for tonight. "Will you do something fun with Jake to get him out of the house this afternoon? Maybe ride bikes or go dig with him in the lot next door?"

"Uh, maybe." His response wasn't very assuring.

"Come on, just for a bit. I don't like you guys on your technology and games all day, it's not good for you. And he loves when you spend time with him."

"Okay, Mom, okay. I gotta go." He stood and walked to the front door where his backpack was waiting for him.

"Love you!" I called as he left.

I headed in the same direction, taking a turn to go down the small hallway toward the kids' bedrooms. Olivia was in the bathroom finishing her hair. She had taken more of an interest in it lately, trying out new fancy braids and hairstyles. Two simple braids deviated from her center part, and she was tying the second one at the end.

"Morning, Liv," I greeted her simply.

"Hi, Mom."

It was easy between us. Something about mother and daughter that made our relationship different than the boys. I'd heard from others this wasn't always the case, that often mothers and daughters didn't get along at all. I hoped that wasn't in our future.

"I saw it's your dinner night. You were planning on tacos, right?"

"Yes," she confirmed.

"Sounds good, thanks Liv."

I headed into the boys' room and had the urge to climb in bed with Jake, but I was sweaty from my ride and run. I knelt by his side and gently shook him.

"Jake buddy, time to wake up."

He didn't even stir. I pulled off his covers, noticing the stuffed dog that had fallen to the side of the bed. He moved slightly as the heat escaped with the comforter.

"Jake, you need to get dressed. What do you want for breakfast? I can make scrambled eggs or toast and cocoa. Which one do you want, bud?"

Muffled groans came from him as he squirmed. I knew he could hear me and was hoping I'd go away.

"Eggs or toast?" I repeated.

"Eggs," was all I got from him. But this was enough, he was awake now.

"Okay, get dressed and come out for breakfast."

I walked back to the kitchen and grabbed the egg carton from the fridge. As I was plating the eggs, I heard his footsteps headed my direction. Olivia was finishing the breakfast strudel she had toasted herself as Jake came in and sat next to her at the small table in the dining nook.

"Juice or milk?" I asked him.

"Juice." One-word answers were all he was ready for this morning. Tonight would be another story. By then he would never have enough of my attention to tell me everything that was inside his head. *Mom, mom, mom!*

Olivia put on her shoes, grabbed her backpack, and was out the door with a quick goodbye. I let Jake turn on the TV for one show while I got myself ready. Luckily, clinic started at nine o'clock, so I could take him straight to school on my way to the University. He'd be early enough to see friends on the playground before the bell, but not too early. Other mornings, my classes started at eight o'clock, and I had to take him to a friend's house to hang out and walk to school together. I knew lots of good people willing to help which I never took for granted.

As I showered, I thought to myself that I had the time to check Facebook and the dating website before I left for the day. If I was going to class, I could check on my laptop during lecture. I did that all the time and my instructors were never the wiser. But today was clinic and it would be busy all day, no time for that. I stepped out of the shower, put my hair up in a towel, and got dressed. Before I started with hair and makeup, I walked over to the laptop and flipped it open. I would check quickly and see what responses I had.

There seemed to be a strong core of supporters that had banded together on Facebook to send me positive vibes and buoy me up. Yes, there were several notifications related to the post from last night. Included were a handful of likes, and comments such as "Dating site for sure," "Homework Schmomework," and "Wait, you're on a dating site?" The last commenter had also sent me a private message, she hadn't gotten the memo that I was now divorced. I sent a message back explaining that yes, I was now dating since Ezra and I had divorced back in August. It was now April, how time flies. I added that we were all doing as well as could be expected though still working out some of the kinks.

With the clock ticking, I closed Facebook and went to the dating website. No new messages. I don't know what I was expecting, I had turned it off late last night and it was early in the day. A girl could always hope, right?

I grabbed socks for Jake and put them on his feet as he was too distracted by the television to do anything himself. I followed with his shoes, then warned him, "Two more minutes." I gathered his lunch, my lunch, and both our backpacks. After loading everything in the van, I returned for the TV zombie.

"We can record the rest on the DVR, but we have to go *now*."

"It's okay." He shrugged. "I've seen this one before."

I dropped him off at the front of the school and went over the schedule. "Remember, you walk home with Joey. Michael and Livvy will already be home."

"I knoooow Mom," he complained.

"Love you!" I chirped as he opened the van door.

"Hate you!" he mimicked my tone affectionately. Every day was opposite day with this kid.

As I drove away, I thought again how lucky I was that the school had allowed him to start first grade this year. He had completed two years of Montessori while I was working on my prerequisites for the dental hygiene program. When I was accepted into the program, I knew it would be like a full-time job. I had been incredibly anxious about what Jake would do in the afternoons since kindergarten was only half day. He was already reading like a champ, so I petitioned the elementary school to allow him to test into first grade. They acquiesced.

Olivia's teacher had brought us in for a meeting a few months into her kindergarten year to have her tested as well. She had been moved to first grade after we discussed all the pros and cons. Sometimes Michael would complain that he was the only one that didn't get to skip any grades, because even I had skipped kindergarten *myself* in a situation like Olivia's. I would remind him how important that year had been for his social growth. He hated hearing that, but it was all too true.

Michael had been on a learning curve for the first few years of school. Well, let's be honest, he was still on it. He couldn't help himself. He knew all the answers and was excited about sharing what he knew with everyone! It had taken longer than it could have. Every other year Michael landed a teacher who understood him and loved him, and on the opposite years it was a teacher lacking the patience and vision he required. The kid was a sponge for facts and information. When we went to the library, he didn't just grab fiction books, he'd bring home books on solar power and nuclear energy. I was eager to feed his interest and guide him safely through his education as best I could from my standpoint as a parent. It was hard when teachers didn't see him like I saw him.

As I walked into the health sciences building at the University, I combed through today's schedule in my head. It didn't take too long. I had two patients—one in the morning, one after lunch. Praise be to the lovely people that were willing to come sit three hours for a dental cleaning. Realistically, they would get halfway through the cleaning then end up coming back for another lengthy visit. Each step of a normal appointment took four times as long with all the documentation, checks and re-checks. It was exasperating, and I felt apologetic for any of my friends that had volunteered their time for my education.

This morning I was in for a treat, Jim was coming in. I'd met Jim at the Masters Swimming practice. Masters was the nice way of saying old people. But the local triathlon group (not "No Excuses") had encouraged a connection with the Masters group as a way to improve swim times for race events. I had become interested when I learned a new "coach" was starting—a coach that was in his early thirties and super cute. He swam in college and knew his stuff, so I figured I could learn a thing or two from him and improve my swim alongside the typical triathletes.

Practice was early on Tuesdays and Thursdays, and I had been ditching the other group those mornings. Several weeks in, Jim had struck up conversation. I think he'd just realized I was single. He had me by a good ten years but was in unbelievable shape. We had become good friends since then. Okay, maybe we'd kissed a couple of times, but I think Jim kept his distance knowing I was a good girl and didn't want to compromise that or our friendship. We spent lots of time together, training and hanging out. He and his brother were ex-military contractors, and just plain fun to hang out with. They were trying to convince me to purchase my first handgun.

"M Dawg!" Jim exclaimed as he grabbed me and pulled me in for a tight hug.

I didn't resist. I could feel the eyes of my three "pod-mates" on us. Each student was assigned to a "pod" of four operatories that shared two sinks and x-ray units. Nothing went on in the pod that the rest of us didn't hear. They were excited to have Jim here too. Last visit, I don't think there was one female that escaped his flirtation, including my instructors. Age didn't seem to deter Jim. He liked all women whether they were the students in their twenties or the instructors who ranged from my age into their early fifties. I led Jim to the patient chair and clipped the bib on him.

"What's going on this weekend?" he asked me.

I debated how to tell him, then decided he wouldn't care. "I have a date on Saturday. I'm going skimboarding."

"Cool," he replied easily. "When? Do we have time for a ride?" Jim wasn't the jealous type. He'd inspired jealousy in others I had dated, but it didn't faze him in the least if I was dating other guys. He always introduced me as a friend. That's what we were. The only thing that bothered him was interference with our training sessions.

"Yeah, we should have plenty of time in the morning. We aren't meeting up till the afternoon."

"Sweet. Do your thing!" He leaned back and rested his head, ready for his three-hour second half of a dental cleaning.

CHAPTER 3
Answered Prayers

As I got out of the van in the garage, I could already smell the taco meat. Olivia had the table set with napkins folded next to each plate. I called to the boys to turn off TVs and computers and join us at the table. I offered a simple blessing on the food, and we dug in.

"So, dance tonight, yes?" I asked Olivia. "I'll clean up while you change."

"Okay," she answered through a mouthful of tortilla, ground beef, cheese, and ketchup.

"Jake, do you want to come with me or stay here?" I asked him.

"Stay here," he mumbled.

Before I could finish my taco, the boys had jumped up and fled the table back to their previous activities. Olivia and I were slower eaters. We chatted about what she had been doing this afternoon, then split up to get dressed and do dishes respectively.

I decided to bring some assignments and work from the van during dance class. Driving back and forth wasted time. Before I pulled out my book, I opened the dating website from my phone. There were a few new messages. These weren't in the chat box for an active discussion, but more like emails to be returned.

The first was an adequate message, but when I checked the profile of the sender, I realized he was a definite no. Same with the second. I didn't think I was a shallow person; however, looks and chemistry couldn't be completely disregarded. The third was nice enough looking but was forty-eight. This was on the higher end of my set parameter. But why did I set it at age forty-nine if I wasn't willing to see? As I read about him on his personal page, I discovered we had some common ground. He was a triathlete, and I liked his style of writing. He was witty and a little sarcastic. It was fun to be around people that challenged me in this way. He was from Alaska, interesting. Why not? I responded to his message, and we'd see where this went with Alaska, 48.

"Time for showers!" I came through the door, already yelling at the boys to shut everything off.

Olivia beat them to the bathroom, but they would be fast when their turns came. I always teased Jake that his showers were so fast that he didn't even get his thick hair completely wet. I couldn't wait until the basement was finished and they had another bathroom. The plan was for the boys to move downstairs and share that bathroom, and Olivia would have her own upstairs. But we were weeks away from that still. I was sick of sawdust and drywall mess; luckily, we were getting to the painting stage now. Who knew how I had accomplished even this much so far in the basement? I was subbing out the work myself, and had the necessary city permits accepted. It had taken multiple tries, but there were many patient subcontractors and city employees that had helped me through it. The paint was scheduled to start on Monday which was a relief.

We gathered in the family room and knelt to say a prayer together before bed. I asked Jake to say the prayer.

"No." He stared at the floor obstinately.

"Come on buddy, it doesn't have to be a big deal. Just think of what we have to be grateful for and what blessings we need. I can help you," I pleaded.

"No," he repeated.

I waited for a long moment before asking Michael to pray

instead. He did so without much protest, and they were off to bed. Homework, study, do it all again tomorrow.

This time as I woke up, I dressed in my swimming suits and pulled sweats over the top. I wore two suits layered on top of each other as the chlorine ate them away and they were too skimpy to wear alone. Spending the money on new suits was silly when I could do this instead. I drove along the quiet roads to the recreation center for Masters practice, listening to my favorite alternative rock station on satellite radio. After a good hour's work in the pool, I was back doing the same thing in reverse. It had been a small group today, but the regulars were present. They pushed me the most so that's all that mattered. Jim was at the pool, but we didn't chat much. He swam in a different lane from me, and we would catch up on Saturday.

Today's class was at eight o'clock. That meant Jake had to be dropped off to walk to school with a friend. I got ready for the day, the older two left for their buses, and I cajoled Jake into the van. As we neared his friend's house he began to cry.

"What's wrong Jacob?" I asked plaintively, using his full name.

"Take me to the school, I don't want to go here today," he demanded.

"Why? What's wrong? You like hanging out with Joey," I tried to persuade him, but I was getting nowhere.

"I just don't want to today," he cried.

Something I had learned about Jake through the separation and divorce was that he hated these moments of handoffs, exchanges, transitions. He didn't know how to express himself in words and would easily break down in tears. It was hard to know how to help him, especially today when I would be late to Dr. Vaunt's class if this didn't resolve quickly. Dr. Vaunt was a former dentist with the Army and very no nonsense. She knew her stuff but could be brutal to late-comers or those who thought they had an excuse to miss class, no matter how important.

"Jake, we can't go to the school yet. It's too early for me to leave you there." I was starting to cry along with him. I didn't want him to see me this way, but it was getting harder to talk through the tears. "I don't know what to do Jacob. What should I do?"

"Just take me to the school," he whimpered.

I texted my friend (as I sat in her driveway) that Jake wouldn't be coming this morning. I drove the two minutes to the school as slowly as I possibly could.

What am I going to do? I spoke to God in my mind—I prayed a lot this way. *How am I supposed to handle this?* I was willing to deal with everything that had been placed in my path and be as cheerful as possible about it, but I couldn't be in two places at once. *Please help me!* I cried out in my mind as quiet tears rolled down my cheeks.

I pulled up to the front door of the school, and as I shifted into park, I saw another minivan pull up behind me. It was a Honda Odyssey like mine but darker gray. It was Tammy. Wait, it was Tammy! Seeing my friend's van was like seeing rain clouds part and the sun shining through. I got out of the van and walked back to her with puffy eyes.

"What's wrong, Melissa?" she asked, concern in her face.

"Jake won't go to Joey's this morning and it's too early to drop him off. What are you doing here so early?" I asked, puzzled.

"Oh, I needed to get some PTSA stuff done and Sam's going to hang out with me." Sam was one of Jake's best friends, we often arranged play dates for them. "Jake can come with us, Sam would love to see him," she said as she walked to my minivan and opened the door, pulling Jake out easily.

Thank you, thank you, I repeated in my mind, knowing this was an immediate answer to my internal prayer. "Tammy, you don't know how much this means to me." I started to cry more as she moved in for a hug.

"It's nothing, really Melissa," she assured as she looked in my eyes. "I'm glad I was here." She walked back to park her minivan and take the boys inside.

It was truly a mini miracle. A tender mercy from heaven. I had experienced many of these lately, and they didn't escape my notice.

I slid into my seat before Dr. Vaunt began her lecture and sighed quietly. My school bestie Samantha was next to me. Actually, she went by Sam. It was funny that both Jake and I had Sams for friends. She was only twenty-two, but we got along well. We were both driven and enjoyed doing projects together.

"How many miles did you do this morning?" she asked under her breath, figuring my sigh came from being tired after a workout.

"Oh, I don't know, I count swimming in yards. That was the easy part of my morning," I responded.

It was all too true. I always laughed a bit at the stress that the other students expressed, because for me school was one of the easier pieces of the puzzle. My workouts were difficult but a moment of freedom and fulfillment. Keeping my kids happy and taken care of was the hardest part. Only two of my classmates had kids and could understand more how I felt, but they weren't single.

As the lights dimmed so we could see the projected slide presentation, the glow of twenty laptops became visible. About half of the students had the lecture pulled up to add notes of their own, and the other half were doing something else. There were lots of social media windows open. I followed suit and opened the dating website. Alaska, 48 had extended an invitation for lunch. I accepted for the following week on a day I knew I would have time.

Then I got a text on my phone. It wasn't as easy to use your phone and not get caught, but a quick glance revealed that it was from Jade. Jade was another single mother whom I had met in Psychology 1010, one of my prerequisites for the Dental Hygiene Department. She had two kids from different dads, life wasn't exactly easy for her either. I liked to buy her lunch now and then, and she would treat me to dinner at a nice steakhouse occasionally. The steakhouse was about thirty minutes away, part of a casino resort just inside the Nevada border. She played virtual poker and was rewarded with resort points, so she would stay in their hotel or take me to dinner to spend them.

I sent Jade a Facebook message so we could communicate on

the computer instead. She wanted to know if I was up for dinner Saturday night. The skimboarding date was scheduled for two in the afternoon, so I thought I could pull it off. Besides, we would be going across the state border and back in time by an hour, so it was totally doable. I told her to meet at my place around six-thirty or seven.

Tonight was karate for all three kids. One class then another. At least Michael and Olivia were in the same class now—it used to be three separate classes! Sometimes Ezra would come and hang out with whichever kids weren't in class at the time and watch the ones who were. It was awkward being around him, so I tried to ignore him and do my homework.

Karate was a great outlet for my kids. I wasn't a big sports fanatic, and neither was Ezra. Plus, I hated the idea of having every Saturday taken up by games. Physical fitness was important to both of us, but we were more into individual sports. We'd always belonged to a club or gym. Even when Ezra was in school and we struggled financially, I worked in the daycare at the gym to earn our memberships.

Olivia was more excited about dance these days and was ready to be done with karate. She was starting to burn out. I'd told her she could quit once she earned her black belt, and she was getting close. Michael had earned his not long ago and Olivia would be eligible in the next round of testing. Jake wasn't with the program most of the time and would often try to leave the mat in the middle of class. The instructors had worked hard with him, spending extra time on motivation and discipline. One day he'd earned a special medal, on another he'd earned five minutes after class of sitting completely still. They knew what our kids were going through and had talked to me about wanting to help us through this tough time. We had such amazing support every direction we turned.

Friday morning was another No Excuses training sesh. This morning we did a trail run up to a beautiful lookout as the day was dawning. These moments were priceless. Being out in nature brought a peace to me that I didn't get indoors. Stephanie brought up the idea of an open water swim, suggesting we do one a week from Saturday. Everyone agreed, and I even volunteered my minivan for transport.

We were only a few weeks away from the Ironman 70.3 race in town, and most of us were involved. 70.3 represented 70.3 miles: 1.2-mile swim, 56-mile bike and 13.1-mile run. It was barely warm enough to start training in the open water for this season, but we had to try it at least once before race day. I wasn't doing the entire 70.3 this year; I had finished the Oceanside, California one in March with No Excuses and I wasn't mentally prepared to do another yet. Not to mention, it was three to four hundred dollars each time for one of these races, just for the entry.

Instead, I was participating on a relay team which was less expensive while at the same time allowing me to be part of the excitement. I was signed up with my friend Janet and her daughter Cassie. I would swim, Janet would bike, and Cassie would run. Janet was one of my good friends and I had really leaned on her the last year. She had three kids the same ages as mine, but also three older kids. Her youngest, Crew, was buddies with Jake.

By one o'clock I was in front of the elementary school, waiting in the long line of cars for the kids to burst forth from the school on their early day. It had been an early day for me as well. As I looked up, I saw Ezra's truck pull into the line. Oh, that's right! How embarrassing, I had forgotten that he wanted to pick up Jacob on his Fridays now. I pulled out of line and drove home to gather up the kids' stuff so it would be easier for them when they got there. Ezra would bring Jake up to grab his things, then go pick up the other two and come back for their belongings as well. It was a lot of driving, but he seemed to like doing the more hands-on dad stuff lately. At first it had bothered me, like he was trying to prove he was a better parent than me. But now I realized it was a blessing that the kids had an active dad in their lives. That wasn't always the case after divorce.

Within an hour and a half, the house was empty, and I was

alone. What was I going to do tonight? With no date scheduled, maybe I'd catch up on homework. Wow, that sounded like a great Friday night! In the past I had scheduled some well-attended ladies only movie nights at my house. But most of my friends were married with kids and couldn't abandon their husbands and families every weekend, nor would I want them to. Other than Jade, I didn't have any single girlfriends.

Maybe I would text Tyler. I had met him through Janet. Tyler had done triathlons and Janet's husband had been training for one, so the three of us had gone out for an open water swim. After that, Tyler and I had gone on a couple of runs together, chatting about our situations. Then a few dates here and there. He was handsome and had a singing voice that made me swoon. But he tended to have fluctuating moods.

Some days Tyler was laid back, others not so much. He was one of the guys that got all jealous over Jim. He'd wanted to go out one night and had texted me, but I wasn't quick to respond because Jim was over. We were just hanging out watching a movie, but still, I'm not rude enough to sit and message someone else like that. So, when I finally got back with Tyler, he'd had a million questions about what I'd been doing and who I'd been with. When he found who it was, he'd become even more upset. I guess he was intimidated by Jim and his fun lifestyle or something, but I didn't see why he was making such a big deal about it since we were just friends. All of us. He knew Jim had a small airplane and that I'd flown with him in it before.

"I guess not all of us can have airplanes," he'd huffed.

Whatever, I didn't need that kind of drama in my life. Okay, maybe I wouldn't text Tyler.

I suppose I'd check out the dating apps I hadn't paid much attention to this week. Swipe around and see what was out there. I had some outstanding messages.

"What's up?"

"Hey, wanna hang out?"

"Hey hottie."

These were trolling messages from days past—guys looking for a quick hookup. I knew these apps could be dangerous, but only if you were reckless. I saw right through these guys and wasn't interested. But despite *them*, occasionally you could find someone pretty cool.

One guy I'd met wasn't half bad. Honestly, in most people's opinions he'd have been the perfect catch. Great looking, wealthy (his family owned a chain of hotels), and very confident. We'd gone out a few times until I finally accepted that it wasn't a good idea. Things had gotten a little steamy one night, and I decided taking chances like this wasn't smart. Especially when I knew there was no way we'd work out. He didn't have an interest in religion anymore, though he'd been very involved his whole life. He'd lost his faith after his wife left him, and now he was floundering. I didn't want to hitch my wagon with anyone like that. My faith was too important to me. We'd kept in touch, but never went out again. Sometimes we would ask each other questions about people we were dating, looking for perspective from the opposite sex.

As I scrolled through the messages, a lengthy one caught my eye. I was curious.

> Looking for a companion who enjoys shopping, travel, and being pampered. I'm married, but my wife and I have an understanding. Our relationship is no longer physical, we stay together for convenience and our children who are older. I would love to take you to Vegas and spoil you. Please say yes.

Disgusting. How did this guy even get the guts to send such a message? Deleted and blocked. I had received one other disturbing message on another app from a husband and wife looking to bring someone else *into* their relationship. It was surprising what was out there. And in this conservative town no less. I was now officially done with dating apps for the night, sufficiently scared away. I could simply watch a movie.

I settled on *He's Just Not That Into You* on Netflix, and when "Friday, I'm in Love" by the Cure came on during the end credits, I spontaneously jumped up and danced around the living room. It felt good to dance. For too many years I'd been a shell of myself. My family had especially noticed this. Melissa was back. I loved not worrying about what anyone thought about me being myself anymore.

CHAPTER 4

When the Kids are Away, Mom Gets to Play

I was at Jim's by seven a.m. It was early enough that we could get in at least a three-hour ride before lunch, and he'd probably make me do a short brick run after also. A brick, from what I understood, was adding in a run after your ride. It was a good way to train your muscles for that transition in a triathlon. I hated running in the heat of the day, but Jim insisted that this was more realistic as to what the temperature would be like on a race day, so I should get used to it. He was good at pushing me and super helpful when it came to nutrition. If nutrition was off, all your training went out the window.

I'd "bonked" before on big rides, one in particular. It wasn't until I was about to collapse that I had figured out what was going on. I had been completely depleted and hadn't taken in enough to compensate for the calories and sweat lost over the past several hours. I'd basically gone into shock, my body shaking and legs cramping up. It so happened that this had occurred as I was going about thirty-five miles per hour down the state park's steep roadway. It was all I could do to get to the bottom of the hill and not crash. As soon as I had been able to safely get off my bike, I had done just that, and immediately sat right on the ground. I had called Janet to come pick me up and told the group I was safe—they could finish their ride. It wasn't until they left that the emotional side had taken over and I'd started crying and shaking all over again.

You would think I had learned my lesson, but it was so tricky to manage the delicate balance of what the body needed. I took salt pills before and during rides to replace electrolytes along with special drink powders and gels. It was a serious business. I was training regularly and intensely enough that I truly considered myself an athlete. That was a word I would never have used to describe myself before. I had always been physically active and enjoyed exercise, but this was a whole new level.

My newfound involvement in triathlon had taken Ezra by surprise. He had offered to buy me a bike before, knowing I had always thought about getting into triathlon. But I hadn't wanted to spend that kind of money while I was busy with school and family. And I'd wanted to devote my time to him and the kids. Of course, once he wasn't around to devote time to and the kids were gone two days a week, there was nothing holding me back. When the kids told their dad I was doing a race, he stammered and stared. *A race?* He looked at me, and I could see him trying to reconcile his idea of who I was with this person he saw me becoming. He had asked me later why I couldn't have been this person with him. Was I really that different? I was still me! But I did have a newfound confidence. I think the fact that he was no longer with me and I was simultaneously gaining confidence was no coincidence.

I was right, Jim forced me to run for twenty minutes after the ride.

"Come on Melissa, can't quit now!"

It was brutal and I wanted to walk but didn't want to disappoint him.

"Push up this hill then it's easy the rest of the way."

Yeah, right, I thought. I didn't even dare voice it. But my stride lengthened as we started the slight decline, and it was definitely feeling good to stretch my muscles this way after the long ride. We made it back and mixed up protein shakes at Jim's house. His brother Brody was home and jovial as usual.

"Yo Mel! When are we going shopping?" He was referring to our earlier conversations about getting a handgun.

"Soon. Maybe in a couple of weeks I'll have more time. I've gotta get through a few things first. But do you guys want to come over for lunch and a movie tomorrow afternoon before the kids get home?"

Of course, they agreed.

Sundays alone were worse than other days because I didn't really go out at all. I went to church, then was home the rest of the day feeling lonely with the kids gone. As part of my religious worship, I set aside the Sabbath as a day of rest and time away from worldly things. But without any family close by it could get hard. Others in my congregation would gather with their extended families, and mine wasn't nearby. I'd followed Ezra around for his education and work, and even though I'd made lots of friends, now I was in a town away from my family. So, Jim and Brody had become family for me lately.

I needed to get home. My date was coming up soon, and I needed to get some food in me and recover a bit before then. I took a hot shower to wash off all the sweat and salt that covered my skin. The desert sun sure did a number on you. Which swimsuit to wear? I was modest, not much of a bikini girl though I had a one or two. I had gotten brave and started swimming in my fitness bikini during the day when I could find the time. I wanted to work on my tan! But it still wasn't comfortable to me, and I didn't like sending any particular signals. I decided on a tankini that brought out the best of my figure and threw a cover-up over it. It was early, so I tidied the house to make it more presentable for tomorrow since I would be busy the rest of the day.

I arrived at the meeting place by the river right on time. I had a picture to go on, but it was a little weird waiting around for someone you had never met before. Luckily, as he approached, Skimboarder,

31 was easy to spot—tall and blonde with a skimboard tucked under his arm. It was hard to believe, but he looked even better in real life. He raised his hand in greeting as he recognized me as well, then waved me over. The path to the river was in his direction. We exchanged pleasantries as we walked and sought out a big rock by the river's edge to set down our towels, my cover-up, and his t-shirt. I'd lived here six years and had never been down to the river. I'd have to bring the kids here, they'd love it.

The river was murky brown, full of sediment from the red dirt that prevailed in this area. It wasn't especially warm since it was April. But if I was any good, I wouldn't have to be submerged in the water. The river was shallow anyway, even with the spring runoff. I hoped I wouldn't get sunburned too badly, but thought I'd gotten that out of the way for the season at my triathlon in California last month.

I'd tried not to stare as he pulled off his t-shirt, because I didn't want to get caught. But now as he was demonstrating the skimboard for me, I soaked in the sights. Man, he looked good. I was drifting away in my thoughts when he handed over the board with a smile.

"Your turn. I'm ready to see what you've got."

"Well now you're making me nervous. Remember, I've never done this before," I responded coyly.

"I have a feeling you'll surprise me," he said and gave me a nudge.

That got my heart racing and gave me some additional confidence. Okay, we'd see how badly I would embarrass myself. Carefully, I started running through the water, tossed the board just in front of me, and jumped for it. I landed too far on one side of the board's back end and immediately felt it slipping. I stepped off quickly, avoiding a fall. I tried a few more times, landing more centrally on the board each time. I didn't coast very far but it was fun feeling the glide.

We walked upriver to a section where there were small ramps and more people. I watched as Skimboarder, 31 did his thing. I was impressed and made sure to tell him so, while touching his arm and glancing at him in just the right way, of course. I think he liked that.

He led me further upriver to a section where the water was dammed and spilling over the top, creating a waterfall. He grabbed my hand and pulled me to the side of the waterfall, and the next thing I knew we were behind it! It was dark with the murky water falling in front of us. He put his hand on the side of my face and leaned in, gently kissing my lips. Though I was surprised I wasn't about to push him away. My face and lips buzzed where he was touching me. I couldn't pretend that I hadn't wondered what this would feel like ever since I saw his picture on the app. His hand slid from the side of my face into my hair. Just as he was pressing closer to me the sound of children approaching pulled us apart.

We emerged from behind the curtain of water, squinting at the change in brightness. Without too much discussion, we headed back downriver to where we'd left our clothes on the rock, toweled off, and covered up.

"Do you have plans tonight?" he asked me as we walked the path away from the river.

I inwardly cursed Jade. "Yeah, I'm going out with a girlfriend later."

"Too bad," he said nonchalantly. "We'll have to get together another time." He leaned in and dragged his lips over mine before finishing with a kiss. As he drew back, I thought he must have seen me leaning forward, almost losing my balance in the moment.

"For sure!" I quickly adjusted my feet and recovered.

I struggled to get my key in the ignition, but eventually got the engine started and pulled out into the street. As I drove, I replayed the last couple of hours in my mind. I was bummed it couldn't continue but knew it may be better to press pause on that moment for now. I needed to be better prepared, mentally, for the next time I saw Skimboarder, 31.

At home I took my time getting showered and ate a snack since dinner was late tonight. Jade made it to my house as I was finishing my makeup. There was a knock on the door, and she pushed it open.

"Mel?" she called.

"In my room!" I hollered. "Come on in!"

She brought in a big bag full of her makeup and hair styling tools. My double vanity was plenty big for both of us.

"I figured I'd finish getting ready here. I just dropped my kids at my mom's."

"No problem." I didn't move from my position, leaning on the countertop so I could see my eyes better to apply eyeliner. "I'm still getting ready, too."

"What have you been up to today?" Jade asked as she pulled out her makeup bag and plugged in her curling iron.

"I went on a ride this morning, then this afternoon I had a date." I smiled, waiting for her reaction.

"A date? With?" I saw her head turn in my peripheral vision.

"This guy that messaged me online. He taught me how to skimboard down on the river."

"Oh yeah?" Her tone suggested that she knew there was more to the story.

"Well…" I gave up the details easily, I was still on a high from the afternoon.

"I swear you meet way more guys than me," she sighed. "How do you find them all?" This did seem somewhat impressive as Jade was seven or eight years younger than me.

"I dunno, I think I'm on all the same sites as you. Maybe it's the age range I'm open to. Try setting yours to forty-nine and see how many messages you get." We laughed, joking about Jade with an older man.

I drove down through the impressive canyon and across the border into Nevada. This was another part of our arrangement; Jade couldn't be frivolous with gas money, so I always drove. The casino was on the south side of the small city, and we went straight to the steakhouse. Most people were on dates or in small family gatherings, we were dressed to the nines and dateless. It wasn't likely we would meet anyone interesting here tonight either as most men who were alone were retired. It was fun to get dolled up anyway.

After dinner, I sat next to Jade as she played video poker. I never gambled. I figured at my age if I had never done it, why start now? Also, I was worried that if I didn't have the perfect record anymore it would be too easy to do it again and again. So, I wouldn't ever have a first time. I had been through this area lots of times while growing up. It was a good stopping point on our way from Utah to California, where my grandparents lived. Sometimes my dad would gamble at night as we slept in the hotel, usually making enough to pay for the rooms and dinner before quitting.

After Jade had enough, we headed out to the van. We had decided against going dancing. There was a little club we liked to go to, but I was pretty wiped out from my day and still had the drive home. I struggled to keep my eyes open driving back up through the winding canyon, even though Jade was gabbing away. My high from this afternoon was gone and I had been up early for the long ride with Jim. When the canyon started to open, I knew it was the last stretch and we would be okay. Jade gathered her purse and high heels as I pulled into the garage. We walked into the house and to the master bathroom for her to collect her makeup and curling iron. She reminded me of something she had been talking about earlier.

"Now that I'm certified, I can bring my massage table over anytime. Let me know when it's a good day for you!" she offered.

I nodded and made a mental note to do this. It would be a good way to support her, and I could really use it. I usually went to a masseuse at the running store. He was especially good at working on my leg muscles that were always bordering on injury, but it was usually painful. I could use a more relaxing massage sometime.

I locked the door behind Jade, waiting for her to drive down the street before turning out the porch lights. I pulled off my clothes and threw them in the hamper. My hair smelled like smoke from the casino, but I didn't have the energy to wash it tonight. I would do that in the morning before church. As my head hit the pillow, I said a bedtime prayer in my mind.

Thank you for keeping me safe on my bike ride this morning and especially driving home tonight, I was beyond tired. Please watch over my kids till I can see them tomorrow night. And I was out.

Church was at nine o'clock, and with no kids to feed or help get ready I could sleep in until just after eight. I really needed it after my late night. I was greeted by several members of the congregation as I entered the church building. I had been attending here for six years, ever since our family had moved from the Midwest. I sat on one of the padded folding chairs toward the back of the chapel to leave the pews for families. I didn't feel awkward anymore after sitting alone like this for over a year.

Church was hard after Ezra first moved out. It seemed that everywhere I looked there were these perfect families and model couples. In contrast, I felt broken. But the more time that went by, I began to see that I wasn't the only one struggling. This morning the Finch's were sitting in front of me. He'd been traveling a lot for work lately and she appeared to be having a hard time with it. I saw her place her hand on her husband's leg. He picked it up and moved it back to her own. Not good, my heart hurt for her.

Not only was I good at noticing things like this now, but I was also being approached quite often by women looking for advice. Some were just unhappy in their marriages. Others had been cheated on or had husbands that sounded emotionally abusive. It was always hard to know how to respond. I usually sympathized with them, validating their feelings. But I made sure they understood that I couldn't give them advice for their marriage as that was very personal. No one could truly understand their situation except themselves.

I had to admit that being at church alone was much easier than with my kids. They were usually pestering each other or talking loudly. For some reason my kids had a difficult time whispering, like they just couldn't figure out how to do it. And then there was the Sunday that Jake had exploded in a tantrum, and I couldn't get him out of the chapel. Unfortunately, we had been sitting toward the front that day. Jake had gotten big enough that I couldn't exactly pick him up and take him out. That meant I had needed to practically drag him down the aisle, with him wailing the whole way.

Jake also had a tough time wanting to go to his Sunday school classes. There were days that I wondered why I even bothered. I kept hoping that God would know I was trying my best and bless me and my kids for our efforts. And I continued to focus on helping my kids gain a foundation of faith in their life that would stay with them.

That Sunday of dragging Jake down the aisle had been particularly difficult. Luckily, I had somehow gotten him to his class after the general worship service. As I had walked down the hall alone, a gentleman stopped me. He was a well-known and respected member of our congregation and the community. He shook my hand and told me that I was his hero. I doubt he would ever know how much that had meant or how long that moment would carry me.

When Jim and Brody came over around noon, we threw steaks on the grill. I mixed up brownie batter and put it in the oven to bake while we ate lunch. Jim and Brody were both currently single, and their mother had passed away from breast cancer several years ago. Needless to say, I think they enjoyed having a woman cook for them. Today was nothing fancy with baked potatoes and steamed broccoli accompanying the steaks, but I had cooked for them before and enjoyed doing it. I think it's because they were grateful and expressed it, which I wasn't used to hearing.

After our meal we found an action movie to watch. I closed the shutters and curtains to try and darken the room in the middle of the bright day. It was kind of early for a movie, but I would be picking up the kids before it got dark. I sent the brothers home with brownies and then headed out to get the kids. They were almost half an hour away now since Ezra had moved into a big house across town. He'd been in an apartment close by originally but was preparing to marry and move his new wife and her children in with him.

It was all pretty weird. Olivia really liked Amber, his fiancé—Amber had taken her shopping and spoiled her. Also, she had an older daughter and I think that was fascinating for Liv. There was a son as well, slightly younger than Olivia, who sounded like a handful. It was going to be interesting to see how this all turned out. I had my doubts about it but played it cool with the kids. It could be painful when they got back from their dad's and Olivia was rambling on about how great Amber was. But what could I say? Making her feel bad for liking her dad's new fiancé wouldn't help anything. Amber seemed to be my opposite with her bright blonde hair and curves in all the right places. I guess I really *wasn't* what Ezra wanted. It hurt, but I was happy with myself and was enjoying my life.

I did worry, however, that this could be a rebound relationship and I really didn't want to see the kids dragged through it. I had already gone through my own rebound of sorts and was still having a hard time forgiving myself. After Ezra had moved out and when I was new on Facebook, I had reconnected with a friend from high school. He was a few years older than me, so we had never dated back then. But he had enjoyed coming over to my house and really liked my family. In fact, he had stayed in touch with them over the years after I was married. After finding each other, we had messaged each other through Facebook consistently for months as he was in another state.

One day it had come to me as clear as anything ever had that I shouldn't be in a relationship with him. I think I had always known that at some level. What had started as a friendship had been developing into more after the divorce and I think he had much stronger feelings for me than I did for him. I truly cared for him, but my emotions had been complicated by my low self-esteem at the time. I'd been very vulnerable. Understandably, he hadn't taken it well when I told him I didn't feel right about continuing a relationship. But I couldn't keep talking myself into it anymore once I knew it wasn't right.

What I had come to recognize in myself and in others was a pendulum swing from who you had been with to your next relationship. I had done that, and I suspected that Ezra was doing it now. Amber wasn't anything like me. And I was concerned that they didn't have the same goals in life which could make family life difficult. Ezra was involved at church and at home with the kids, studying scriptures and saying prayers as a family. It sounded like this was different from Amber and her kids, so it could eventually put a strain on their relationship. Only time would tell.

Waiting for the kids on Ezra's porch was strange. I perceived that even looking inside the house was regarded by him as a huge invasion of privacy. The kids could feel it too, at least the older ones. Jake was trying to tell me about the new house and show me things, and I was trying to avoid it and move him toward the minivan. They caught me up on their weekend as we drove home. There hadn't been much time for fun, but they managed to race go-carts at some point. Their dad had been busy helping Amber pack and move with the wedding this Wednesday. Good luck to all of them—blending this family wasn't going to be a cakewalk.

CHAPTER 5
Letting Go and Holding On

Monday morning was a run and swim with No Excuses, then getting the kids off to school and myself to clinic. The dental hygiene program was like a full-time job, only I paid tens of thousands of dollars for them to basically own me. I was lucky because Ezra had left a big nest egg that was paying for most of it. He'd been putting it aside for me the past several years which I was grateful for. I'd been debating dipping into the savings to help with the basement finishing costs. I owned the house now and wanted to get it done so I could sell it easier one day. And for more of a profit. Besides, in the meantime the kids really needed more space.

I dashed home on my lunch hour to meet the finish carpenter that was starting work on the basement. He had walked around back and let himself in through the basement sliding door like I had asked him to.

"Hello." He extended his hand and smiled as he looked me up and down in my scrubs.

"Sorry, I only had a quick lunch break to come meet you," I apologized as I shook his hand.

"Not at all, are you a nurse?" he asked.

"Nope, I'm in dental hygiene school."

"And your husband is making *you* take care of business?" he asked in a way that I sensed was exploring my relationship status.

Maybe it was because I wasn't wearing a ring. That or he could just tell—somehow, I knew I sent a different signal now. He had a playful, flirty way of communicating and would be working at the house through the next week. Intriguing.

"No husband," I answered. "Just me in way over my head trying to get this basement finished."

This signal I sent made me nervous sometimes. I worried that a married guy would get the wrong idea. I invented disturbing scenarios; one involved a woman at church accusing me of trying to steal her husband. I had no intention of ever flirting with any married men, it horrified me to think about it. Being single took some getting used to.

Alaska, 48 had the flirting down as well. I met him the next day in jeans and a fitted t-shirt for our lunch date. Luckily, today was not a scrubs day at school. We met at a Hawaiian restaurant near the University campus. Doing the usual divorcee thing, we shared the highlights of our stories, explaining how we had become single again. I could tell right away that Alaska had some baggage. So did I, but he seemed unsure about women and their motives in general. He passed all his commentary off as jokes, but it was plain to me that it was from being burned by his former wife, and maybe other women after. Still, I enjoyed our conversation. He was intelligent and interesting. I'd go out with him again if he asked, which I thought he would.

I had started noticing a strange energy about me, knowing what was around the corner. It was Ezra and Amber's wedding. The kids had told me they weren't having a big wedding, no reception or anything. They were simply going to the courthouse. All Ezra had told me was what time he would pick them up. Jake had been complaining that he didn't want to go, and his dad seemed to play down the whole thing like it was no big deal. He told Jake he didn't even have to dress up.

Then Thursday afternoon Ezra was on my porch holding a set of church clothes for Jake. Immediately Jake lost it. He started crying and ran into the family room where I was, collapsing in my lap. I couldn't talk him through any of it. He wouldn't communicate except to say no and cling tighter to me. I called to Ezra and said he needed to come in so we could talk with Jake together. He refused to enter the house. He hadn't been inside since the day he had moved out. I'd tried at the beginning to have him come to the kids' birthday dinners but soon got the message that he didn't want to be there in *my* house.

After several more minutes he relented and walked in. This was an emergency. I mean he was getting married soon, I was guessing, though I didn't know when it was scheduled. Together we calmed him down, Ezra promising it wouldn't be like one of those boring church weddings. *It would be quick*, he said. Inside this killed me, he didn't seem to understand what was going on with Jake. Did he think this was about putting on church clothes and being bored? Couldn't he see what it was really about? This six-year-old knew his parents were done for good now. Jake had always tried to push us together in situations and he was getting the full picture now. Michael and Olivia had hung back staying out of the way of this implosion, but now they headed out the door together. I guess Jake would dress in the car.

I closed the door behind them and finally allowed my emotions to take over. I had to be strong for my kids, but they were gone now so I could let it out. I didn't mourn the loss of my marriage, that was long over. I wasn't even upset he was getting married. Well, okay, maybe there were a few tears for those things. But mainly it was my kids I was crying for—it was painful for me to watch Jake hurt like that. I knew the older two had their own concerns as well. And I could see there was a long road ahead in blending this family and I couldn't protect them from any of that.

I didn't allow myself to wallow for too long. The kids would be coming home tonight after all, and I wouldn't want them to see me this way. On occasion they caught me, but I had literally bitten my tongue to keep back tears at other times. I was glad I had calmed down because they were home much sooner than I'd expected. I don't even know how they had time for a proper meal let alone the actual wedding. But according to the kids' accounts it had been a very quick and awkward ceremony at the courthouse. I was surprised when Ezra mentioned he'd be at Olivia's black belt testing on Saturday. No honeymoon? Maybe later, not my business.

That evening it was my turn to say the family prayer. I said that we were thankful the kids could go to their dad's wedding. I requested extra blessings for everyone as they moved into the house together and got to know each other better. It was important to me to show my kids that if I could do this, they could. I'm not sure they got that message, but I hoped they would.

As part of my own prayer before bed, I expressed gratitude that Jake had calmed down and made it to the wedding. I also asked for help to get all four of us through this transition. And I thanked God for keeping me strong.

The No Excuses open water swim was on Saturday. The kids could watch cartoons and have a leisurely morning when they woke. I was leaving early and wouldn't be too long. Everyone piled in my van with their swim gear. We weren't going to have a repeat of the last time I drove this group to an open water swim. This time we were going to a different reservoir to avoid Swimmer's Itch.

Last year we had broken all the rules without knowing it: we swam parallel to the beach, the wind was blowing towards shore, and we hadn't toweled off right away. Luckily, we had been wearing wetsuits which had blocked most of the little parasites that burrowed into your skin and died, causing a terrible itch and even hives for some. As we had driven home that day, we had scratched at an increasing rate. Jenny had been wearing a sleeveless wetsuit, and for the next week had looked like she had the chicken pox.

I still swam out there with the local triathlon club on Wednesday evenings through the summer, but we took precautions. We swam straight out from the shore and always toweled off immediately after. I never got the dreaded Itch a second time.

The other reservoir was not as picturesque which meant it wasn't as crowded. That was a plus. Less boats also meant safer conditions. The swim was a success and I got home in time to make some late breakfast for the kids.

That afternoon was Olivia's black belt test. Michael had advice for her, but she didn't seem to listen much. I was going to do the run portion with her. They were required to do a fitness test of running, push-ups, lunges, and sit-ups in the early afternoon. The weapons demonstrations, grappling, and sparring matches would follow in the evening. Liv made it through the fitness portion like a champ. My favorite part of the evening was watching her high kicks to her sparring partner's head. Luckily, they wore padded helmets, and she didn't kick too hard anyway. She was very flexible, and it showed in the kicks and splits. This was also helping her in dance class.

The black belt ceremony was fun to watch. The new black belt recipients got to have a fun grapple with their lead instructor. Olivia climbed on his back when he was down on the mat, putting him in a chokehold. He gave her a tap, tap on her arm to show she had bested him, then whipped her upside down by her feet to show he could still get her. After they had all taken their turns, they lined up and took off their striped belts so he could tie on their new black belts. I was happy that Olivia had stuck with it and made it to this point.

Ezra picked up the kids late Sunday afternoon. We had joint custody, but with his work schedule he wasn't available to have them half of the time. Basically, he had them two nights a week—either Friday and Saturday or Sunday and Monday. So, this time they would be back to me after school on Tuesday. Tonight, I would get organized for my week and Monday after clinic I would have my solo date at my favorite Thai restaurant.

This dinner out had become a regular event for me, and I looked forward to it. I always ordered the panang curry and a Dr. Pepper with the good pebble ice. I would eat about half the bowl of curry, then they would get me extra rice to take home for leftovers along with a Dr. Pepper to go. I'm sure they felt bad for me, eating alone every other Monday, but I loved it. It wasn't awkward for me to be alone; I had even gone to a couple of movies by myself. I didn't *always* like it, but after fifteen years of marriage and someone always needing something from you, it could be a nice break.

After my solo date, I arrived home with the plan of getting ahead on my schoolwork for the week. But when I got a message from Skimboarder, 31 that all went out the window. He basically invited himself over and I didn't see a problem with that. He seemed like a decent guy. When he arrived, I led him into the kitchen and pulled out ice cream options. We sat at the kitchen table and chatted as we ate, getting to know each other better.

Eventually we moved into the family room and sat down on the couch. He didn't waste any time, leaning in and wrapping his hand around the back of my head to pull me toward his face. He was a good kisser, no question about it. After a minute or two he laid my head back onto the arm of the couch and shifted to reach my lips from above me. As he pressed closer, I heard a crinkling sound coming from his pocket. I'm not sure why, but I was suddenly very interested in what this was. I thought I had an idea.

"What's in your pocket?" I stopped his progress toward me.

"Huh? Nothing." He was caught off guard but obviously avoiding something.

I shamelessly started to reach into his pocket.

"Okay fine, here." He moved my hand and pulled out a condom from his jeans pocket.

"Wait, you really thought that was happening tonight?" I exclaimed in surprise.

He shrugged in response.

"Look, this isn't a good idea." I was adamant. "I'm not having sex with you or anyone, not until I'm married. I don't know what impression I gave you, but it's *not* happening." I stood up and he slowly followed suit. "Sorry, I like you, but this isn't going to work."

He tried to protest that he didn't expect anything, that we could just spend time together. I knew that he would always have it in the back of his mind, and I didn't need that pressure. I let him out, locked the door, then turned on the TV for some noise and distraction—I was jittery and anxious. Pacing while I flipped through the channels, my stomach finally settled. After watching the end of a *Golden Girls* episode, I was calm enough to get ready for bed. It was too bad. He was cute and fun, but I wasn't taking that risk.

The kids came home the next day, and the week went by quickly in the usual fashion. School, karate, dance, and lots of workouts. Wednesday evening open water swims had started up at the reservoir, and I joined the triathlon club for that event. Friday after school the kids headed back with their dad for the next two nights. Again, I didn't have plans for Friday, but I truly needed to focus on school. My finals were this next week, so I had to buckle down and study. Besides Monday with Skimboarder, 31 I hadn't had any other dates, not that I could call that a date. I did talk a little with the finish carpenter. The kids had even come down to the basement to see what was going on after I had been there for a long time. They had seen the way we interacted as we talked to each other. Olivia had come up with a nickname for him on the spot, or maybe it was Michael. Either way the name stuck—Flirter Number One.

Saturday, I went on a long ride with No Excuses. Then after a nap I headed to the dance club with Jade and her friends. I was the designated driver since I didn't drink. That and my minivan could hold everyone. I got some special attention at the club from a Latin American who was a good dancer with a sexy accent. Jade kept a close eye on me, ready to swoop in and give him the brush-off for me if needed. But I was having a good time. By the end of the evening, one of the girls in our group was beyond tipsy. She was struggling to walk and was very confused and upset that we were driving home in a minivan. She lost a shoe at some point, and I was concerned she would throw up on the way home—we still had the canyon to drive through. Luckily, we made it without any issues, and I got everyone dropped off and home myself.

Finals week flew by without a hitch, and I kept my position on the Dean's List. I had officially completed one year of dental hygiene school, which was no small feat. We had grown close as a class; twenty women bonded together through time, tears, and exhaustion. I was grateful to have the tests out of the way so I could prepare mentally for the big day.

CHAPTER 6
Compromise

Thursday afternoon our team had checked in at the Ironman athlete village located in the park next to the library. They had fastened wristbands on Janet, Cassie, and me which would give us access to athlete-only areas on race day. We had taken pictures together and checked out the t-shirts that were available to purchase. A free t-shirt came with our swag bag at registration, but it wasn't as nice as some of the others. One shirt for sale had the names of all the hundreds of participants in small print on the back. We'd searched until we found our names, then I'd bought one.

I took the kids with me to the athlete village the next day so they could see the excitement. Participants were checking in their bikes and gear bags that would be staged at transition areas. There was a panel of professional triathletes and there were booths to check out. I wished the kids could be with me on race day, but I couldn't keep track of them during my swim portion. They wouldn't have fun the way I did anyway. They were going to stay with their dad Friday night and come back to me Saturday evening.

Race morning, I was up by four a.m. and my stomach wasn't happy about it. I always got race day stomach, complete with extra bathroom trips and a little nausea. I made myself have a protein shake and brought other food to munch on before the swim. Janet was at the reservoir early as well since she'd be doing the bike portion after the swim. We chatted with others near our designated T1 (transition one) spot where Janet's bike hung. I pulled my wetsuit up to my waist, leaving it off the shoulders for now and keeping on my jacket. I strapped the timing chip on my ankle then paced to calm my nerves. We weren't trying to win anything, but I got like this with every event. The swim had its own reasons for causing this nervousness. There were wave starts by age group which broke up the crowd somewhat. Still, it could get sketchy out in the water, especially at first till it thinned out. Also, it was barely getting light, and the water was uncomfortably cold. I had to stick my face in that!

The different groups started assembling, moving slowly toward the swim start. I set my jacket in my gear bag and worked the wetsuit up over my shoulders so Janet could help zip it up. I tugged the neon swim cap over my head, trying not to pull my hair out in the process, then grabbed my goggles.

"Good luck Melissa, you've got this!" Janet gave me a quick squeeze.

There was music playing over big speakers, and the blue sky was overtaken by ribbons of flame as the sun came closer to rising over the mountain. My stomach turned and my heart raced as the wave of athletes in front of me swam out to the starting buoy. The horn sounded and they took off. I ditched my flip-flops, dollar ones I would never see again. I stepped into the water, pulling my goggles down over my eyes. I swallowed a gasp as the shock of cold water leaked through my wetsuit zipper—my tough exterior wouldn't betray me to the surrounding athletes. I swam several strokes with my head above the water before taking the plunge. At the buoy we tread water waiting for the start signal.

The blaring sound of the horn sent the calm water into a churning frenzy. Usually, in a triathlon swim I would conserve my leg strength and rely mainly on my arms. But since I was done after the swim, I wasn't concerned about that. I kicked hard, trying to separate myself from the melee. The first five minutes were almost a sprint, but as I pulled away from the pack I settled into a rhythm. My arms were strong enough to keep up a quick pace for this 1.2-mile distance. Usually, I could swim it in thirty to thirty-five minutes. I alternated my breathing between sides. Right, left, right with my arms and breathe on the left. Left, right, left and breathe on the right. Intermittently I would raise my head briefly to spot and make sure I was heading in the right direction. One or two strokes and my head was back down. I passed a few swimmers from previous wave starts. I could identify them from their different colored caps. As I rounded the last buoy, I picked up the pace, kicking harder again and sprinting into the finish.

I had learned not to touch the bottom early and walk in, but to swim until you were forced to put your feet down. Swimming was faster than walking through the water. I yanked off my goggles but left on my cap and wetsuit, jogging by the volunteers who would help you strip off your wetsuit. I had been one of those volunteers the year before.

I found Janet and she grabbed the timing chip off my ankle and strapped it onto her own, yelling a "good job!" as she hustled her bike to the area where she would be allowed to mount, clip in, and begin the fifty-six-mile ride.

I went to our transition space and took off my wetsuit. I toweled off then walked back to where I could see the swimmers running down the chute to their bikes. I stayed there until the last swimmer exited the water and the swim time was cut off. I wanted to cheer on everyone I knew that was racing. Most wore identifying race kits, and I knew many that were part of our triathlon club. Then I pulled on my sweats, gathered my things, and went home to shower.

The hot water chased away the shivers I had been battling and soothed me after the anxiety of the morning. I dried my hair slightly and applied light makeup, then dressed in a dry race kit. Time was counting down as I reached the T2 transition area in the middle of town. Janet would be arriving soon, and Cassie would start the run.

I learned from the online athlete tracker that my swim had

been just over thirty-one minutes—pretty good. I could see the checkpoints Janet had passed and knew she would be arriving soon. Cassie and I waited together as she did her own pacing, waiting for her turn. We both cheered when we saw Janet dismount and jog her bike in. I unstrapped the chip and fastened it around Cassie's ankle, and she was gone. I whooped a little for her, then turned to Janet to tell her how awesome she did. She was sweaty and panting, and I asked if she needed her water as she pulled off her helmet and gloves. She said she was ready to go sit down, so I suggested the athlete tent knowing they would have food ready for us. We headed over and grabbed salty chips, a sandwich, and a drink. They even had cookies! We sat and she broke down her ride, telling me the details.

After eating, we met up with Janet and Cassie's family and watched the professional women cross the finish line. It was incredibly inspiring to see them. Part of Janet's family left to go see Cassie at one of the points she would pass by. The rest of us hung out there, a lot was going on and there was a festive mood. When we knew Cassie was closing in, we went to the finish line. We were allowed to wait there so we could be together as she crossed. When we saw her, we started screaming her name, and she ran straight to us and into our open arms. Volunteers gave us finisher medals and hats and we took pictures together. I loved being in that moment. We had all done something hard that day and had made a good team. Being surrounded by all the athletes and spectators was energizing. I soaked it in as we took Cassie back to the tent to get her some food.

Then we went our separate ways to head home. I could've spent all day out there, but my kids would be coming back soon, and I needed down time first. We hugged again and it took me another half hour to get to my car as I kept stopping to talk to friends along the way.

When they arrived at home, the kids asked how the race had gone. I showed them pictures from the reservoir, transition areas, and with our team at the finish. They acted proud, but they didn't really understand much about what I did with triathlon.

They'd been at my first triathlon; the event had been at a fitness club and my parents had come down to be there with them and watch as well. My dad was my inspiration, he'd done a few triathlons when I was young. He'd taken some great action pictures of me while the kids held posters and cheered with my mom. My dad was a professional photographer, his second career after retiring from dentistry. He'd been my inspiration for dental hygiene school as well.

I took inspiration from my mom in other ways, namely music and parenting. In college I had sung in the Utah Symphony Chorus with her. And she was the reason I had delivered all three of my children naturally. Watching her calmly labor during childbirth had been awe inspiring. She'd worked with the kids to make the posters ahead of time. I was happy to have them all there that day.

The only other spectator that had come to my races was my sister Leah. She'd come for my first Olympic distance triathlon with her kids. They had been there for the finish, and she was an angel to apply aloe vera on my back after I'd been terribly sunburned. She'd also been at the finish of the first half marathon I did. I stayed in her home the nights before and after the run. She'd carb loaded me with delicious pasta the night before and was at the finish with her family.

Most of the time though, when I did events, I was hanging out with other amateur athletes. We enjoyed these adventures together and understood the drive and determination it took. In a very real way, triathlon had helped save me this past year.

When I woke the next morning, I waited in bed to see what the kids were up to for Mother's Day. I had always enjoyed this day. In fact, I'd never heard that there were mothers that *didn't* enjoy it. Then last year I'd been introduced to that population that did indeed exist. Suddenly there was a day to be reminded about everything that was amiss in my life and to make me feel like I wasn't measuring up as a mother. But the kids had done such a good job of taking over the day's duties and we had all enjoyed it.

The door opened and Michael and Jake brought me handmade cards, Jake jumping into bed with me to give me a snuggle. In the hallway was a banner made of small hearts strung together spelling "Happy Mother's Day".

Olivia made me stay put, she had prepared breakfast in bed for me. On the center of a baking sheet was an ivy decorated Corelle plate with a large pancake. In true Olivia presentation the pancake had a face on it with fried eggs for eyes, an English muffin with strawberry jam as a nose, and a bacon smile. There were two drink options—a strawberry smoothie and apple juice. The place setting was completed with salt and pepper and silverware wrapped in a napkin. She also had hand-crafted paper flowers in a bud vase with a note attached.

I praised all three for making me feel special, but the day wasn't over. At church the children sang to the mothers, and they brought pie to the women's class as well. Once home, Michael had another treat for me.

"Mom, lay down on the floor for your massage!"

I followed his instructions, and Jake even jumped in to help with whatever Michael wasn't working on. All three kids helped with dinner and clean-up, and though I knew I wasn't a perfect mother, I sure loved these beautiful souls and how they wanted to spoil me. It was hard not to find joy in the day, broken as I felt our family was.

With the kids still in school and my own schedule freed up, I had more time for dating. I arranged as much during the daytime as I could. I was always surprised that these men had such flexible schedules and could make the time for it. I had another lunch with Alaska, 48 and a bike ride as well. We had a good time together. Flirter Number One got in touch and invited me for a ride on his Harley Davidson. That was a new adventure for me, and I loved it. Another day we went out in his covered off-road vehicle to sand dunes near the reservoir. He had me scared, launching off the tops of dunes, catching air. It was like a rollercoaster!

Alaska, 48 fed my mind and Flirter Number One kept me entertained with adventures. They were attractive but in different ways. They both had daughters and understood what it meant to have a family. I had chemistry and felt safe with each of them, like I would be taken care of and loved. But neither seemed right.

I was getting quite a bit of attention lately on the dating apps and websites also. I think men really liked how I did triathlons. There had been some entertaining date offers. One guy was young, handsome, and just headed to graduate school. Not a chance—been there done that with Ezra. Some older men had asked me out, men in their late fifties and even early sixties. They said they had a hard time finding women their age that were as active as themselves. Sorry, not happening. Then there was the dairy farmer. I was convinced from his picture that he was from a polygamous community and looking for a second wife. His message was kind but made me laugh.

> Would You be interested in exploring a friend ship? If so, would You be interested in Me taking You for a tour of a excellent and large (4200 cow) high tech dairy operation, where I am working and based at this time. And perhaps taking a four wheeler ride up a small mountain close by (about 4 miles) that provides a good view of the area, and perhaps going out to dinner.? What do You think?

I had another triathlon coming up in a few weeks, but my training was pretty much the same all the time. I signed up for my first century ride; the century meant it was over a hundred miles. And the event I was most excited for this summer was a swim marathon, a 10k swim in Northern Utah. I was required to bring my own kayak support and Jim was game.

Jim and Brody finally got me to decide on a handgun. I chose a Smith & Wesson M&P Shield. The grip was comfortable, and it was easy for me to handle. Jim and Brody both open carried their handguns and extolled the virtues of doing so. I was fine with *them* doing it but not interested in that myself, nor did I want a concealed carry permit. I just liked target shooting and having a gun in my home that I was comfortable using. They taught me how to assume a defensive stance for shooting and let me try out their semi-automatic and sniper rifles when we went out to shoot. They loved how much space the minivan had when I put the seats down, though it rode low when it was loaded with all those weapons and ammo.

One weekend the kids were away I went boating with Flirter Number One and his friends. I even met his teenage daughters. Taking a turn on the kneeboard for the first time in forever, I wowed them all with a 360. I hadn't really done any of my favorite things in over fifteen years. Ezra didn't seem to like anything to do with water or sun, and I hadn't snow skied for years either. I couldn't blame it entirely on him. For one thing, we had been young, poor, and focused on getting his education finished, bouncing all over the country. And we had been raising little ones who made it more difficult to do these things. But also, these were compromises I made when I married Ezra.

I had gone through the pendulum swing before after dating lots of fun but irresponsible guys in college. When Ezra had come along and had a plan for his life I had been impressed. I had decided we didn't need to have everything in common if our main goals were in sync. We were both dedicated to God and wanted to raise our children in faith. Education was important to both of us, and we focused on that with our children.

Now, hanging out with Flirter Number One and his crew I wondered if this had been wishful thinking. Did spouses need more in common? And although we were on the same page with almost everything to do with our kids, the problem was that everything with Ezra and I had always been about the kids. From my perspective it had never been about us and our relationship. That was a compromise I wouldn't make again.

After the day of boating, we went back to Flirter's house, and he built a fire in his backyard fire pit. He smoked delicious meat and fed us, then we hung out and talked. I could get used to this kind of life. He worked hard, but he knew how to play too. He was a good family guy and cooked! Flirter Number One had left religion after becoming disenchanted with the religious community he had grown up in. Faith didn't have a role in his life anymore, but he was a good person. I was starting to question everything I had been holding out for.

I drove home that night agitated and confused. Would I ever be able to find someone who could fill all my needs—did such a person even exist? I dissolved into tears as pain grew in my chest. I was lonely. I wanted a partner for all areas of my life. Dating was fun but not enough. How long could I do this and not lose my determination or become depressed? Was it possible to stay that "good girl" I had always tried to be?

I called out to God in my mind and in my heart. *Will I ever find the man for me? Is he out there?* I pulled over and let the sobs rack me. I was exhausted and angry, blaming Ezra for putting me in this position. I questioned God, asking him if this would ever be made right.

I felt adrift in this new life. I pictured myself aboard a small boat, being pulled out to sea after having the mooring ropes severed from the safety of the dock. The wind and waves of the open ocean threatened to swallow me whole, and I was desperate to stop the progress of my drifting. Starting the engine, I turned the boat into the wind that was driving me outward. But to no avail. The wind was stronger and faster than the engine. I rushed to the front of the boat, and finding the anchor, heaved it with all my might into the ocean. I tied the anchor's rope to the cleat and waited. The bow of the boat was being pushed sideways by the wind and I worried all hope was lost. Then the anchor found the sand and latched onto a rock on the bottom of the ocean, snapping the bow back toward the wind and halting the seaward progression. I remained safe in the harbor.

Slowly the pain in my chest dispelled as a feeling of peace and calm took over. My heart burned in confirmation of thoughts that had come into my mind. *Yes, this will be made right. Have faith and patience, you will have more than you ever had before. He is out there waiting for you. Rest in me until the time is right.*

My tears of anguish transformed into tears of gratitude. I could not doubt what I was feeling. God knew me and had a plan for me. I was not adrift as long as I was anchored in Him. I could never deny this moment and what I had felt. I thanked God for giving me exactly what I needed to know. I wouldn't doubt Him anymore—He was my strength on the water.

CHAPTER 7
Summer Days

It was officially summer! In addition to the pool trips and outdoor activities, I always liked doing something educational to keep the kids busy. One year we had created weekly newsletters and Michael and Olivia had written articles and book reviews for it. We'd added lots of pictures and highlighted the fun things we'd been doing, then printed them out and sent them to grandparents, aunts, uncles, and cousins. Last year we had celebrated an international summer. Each week we had focused in on a different country or part of the world. We'd gone to the library and checked out books about the country of the week then cooked meals from there as well.

This summer was more laid back. We were exploring different non-fiction sections of the children's library. I would never have known, for example, that there was an entire section on paranormal and alien activity. We found books of ghost stories and other phenomena and read them together at home.

My next triathlon was on the last day of May and some of Jim's friends came down for the event. While a few did the Olympic distance, I did the sprint: a 750-meter swim, 12.4-mile bike and 3.1-mile run. After the race I invited the gang to my house to have dinner together. We had a good time hanging out and planned to do a longer distance triathlon together up on their turf in August.

We took all the obligatory before and after pictures, but my favorite picture may have been the one I took in my finisher tee. I had a good collection now of finisher t-shirts. They were tangible bragging rights earned by completing the event. I had a matching collection of medals but didn't know what to do with them, so I just kept them on a hanger in my closet.

A couple of weeks later I took the kids to Zion National Park, and we did a short hike. The boys liked to run ahead and explore, and Liv and I hung back taking lots of selfies and pictures in general. We all played in the river, and I had the cutest picture of Michael giving me a kiss on the cheek as we waded.

This picture was especially sentimental for me because Michael struggled with the divorce. It seemed that he thought he had to take sides. Sometimes I'd get caught up defending myself, but I usually tried to stay calm and not engage. I had tried explaining to him how lucky he was to have two parents that loved him, and he didn't have to choose one of us. He could love us both just like we both loved him. I knew he loved me. He had a sweet way of coming up behind me and pushing my tense shoulders down as a reminder to relax, massaging my neck and shoulders.

This year I had purchased season tickets to the outdoor amphitheater. They produced amazing musicals and shows, and I got five tickets so we could always invite an extra with us. The shows for the season were *The Wizard of Oz*, *The Little Mermaid* and *Joseph and the Amazing Technicolor Dreamcoat*. The productions were phenomenal and being outside in the red rock canyon added to the ambiance. *The Wizard of Oz* was first in mid-June before it got too hot. The other two shows were in the fall.

The Wizard of Oz was well done. I invited Alaska, 48 to join us and introduced him as a friend to the kids, which he was. I couldn't see us progressing further in a relationship. The kids begged for all the treats at the show, and I gave in for one each. But I drew the line at the expensive trinkets for sale. There were big painted boards of the show's characters with holes where their faces belonged. The kids climbed up behind the boards and put their faces through the holes for pictures, making silly faces. Alaska, 48 was good at joking with the kids but neither he nor the kids got too involved with each other.

A few first-date-only's had come and gone recently. It could be difficult to let a guy down gently! I tried to be nice and give a hug at the end of the date, and certain men translated that as grounds for a second date. I was constantly surprised at guys who couldn't read body language. Or maybe they were simply brave because they had a hard time taking no for an answer. But I only had so much time and didn't owe anyone anything besides common decency.

Toward the end of June, the kids were with their dad for two weeks. It was well-timed since I had some plans. First was a dental hygiene convention in Las Vegas, which was fun because I got to spend time with my classmates removed from school. We attended continuing education classes, laid by the pool, saw the Blue Man Group, and ate out. I really wanted to go dancing and was surprised when all the girls wanted to stay back and go to bed early. I was almost the oldest of the class! Not even my closest hygiene pal Sam would go with me. Luckily, I finally coaxed Taylor.

Taylor had a reputation of partying so I knew I could convince her, but I didn't know what I was getting myself into. This girl was a natural at pulling guys in, and before long we had been invited to join a group at a table. I wasn't drinking, of course, but it was fun to have people to hang out and dance with.

After about an hour, the table next to us was getting rowdy. They were a hockey team and had been playing in a tournament. I don't know what set it off, but the next thing we knew the guys in our group were tangled with the hockey team and punches were being thrown. Taylor took me by the hand and pulled me away—she was much more street smart than me. As we neared the exit, we saw security headed toward the fight.

We made our way down the strip to where we were staying at the Paris, and I couldn't take my high heels anymore. I knew it was disgusting, but I pulled them off and walked barefoot, avoiding the pornographic advertisements littering the sidewalks. My shins ached, and my feet were blistering on the backs of my heels. I hoped my feet and legs would recover quickly because in two days I was running a 5K.

The next morning, I packed and drove north to my parents' home. As the oldest of eight I had been distant for too long. The year before Ezra had dropped the divorce bomb on me, I had become motivated to spend more time with my family. It was like getting to know them all over again. I had lived far away for years, and in the meantime, they had grown up. But in the last year and a half, being close to my family had been essential for my life transition.

This 5K race was an extended family event, and a few of my siblings should be there. My cousin had created a foundation for his daughter who had passed away from childhood cancer. The foundation held an annual run and donated the proceeds each year to two or three children and their families to help with their expenses from cancer treatments.

My mom was happy to see me when I arrived at her home.

"Melissa, you look great! But maybe tired? What can I get you to eat?" She couldn't help herself—she was a mother through and through.

"I'm fine mom. What leftovers do you have?" I asked.

"We have Chinese from the other night or cabbage soup I made a few days ago. Or we can make something else, a salad or sandwich?" she kept offering options.

"The soup sounds wonderful, thank you. I *am* pretty tired." I laid down on the couch as she reheated the soup. It was in a tomato-based broth and was just right after eating out too many times recently.

We discussed the schedule for the next day. My brother Daniel and his wife would be traveling down with us, some others in their own cars. After I finished eating, we visited a little longer, then I turned in early knowing we would be *up* early as well.

The run was held at a large park in Salt Lake City and a good portion of the runners were dressed up as it was a "Princess" run. I wore a simple tiara with my running skirt. Princess characters in attendance included Ariel, Cinderella, and Belle. There was a fun family presence, and it was nothing like the other events I participated in. I ran the 5k in just over twenty-seven minutes, so barely under a nine-minute pace. That was fine with me. Not only were my feet killing me from the dancing and high heels a couple of nights before, but I wasn't trying to prove anything. Nor could I if I wanted to, I wasn't a natural runner. I was there to support family and enjoy myself.

After the race, the family was all invited to my uncle and aunt's home to swim in the beautiful pool at their estate. It was fun to catch up with everyone. I had over thirty cousins on this side of the family, my mom's side. She was one of seven children. I had spent more time with these cousins because I'd grown up nearer to them. My dad was the oldest of three. His sister was in California and his brother had been in Florida for years. I only had my two grandmothers now since I'd lost my grandfathers in the last few years.

I took a turn on the diving board, using the approach I had been taught when on the summer diving team nearly twenty-five years ago. I couldn't do anything fancy but could make a simple dive look decent. I bounced almost straight up off the board. Then bending down in a pike position, I grasped my ankles. Unfolding again, I kicked my feet up and entered the water as streamlined as possible. My hands were folded inside each other over the top of my head. My cousin captured it on camera, and I posted it later that day on Facebook. I couldn't help sharing because it was a perfectly timed picture. It got plenty of likes and comments.

My favorite was, "You've got to be kidding me. You dive as perfectly as you swim."

"That diving team experience has stayed with you, I am glad!" my mom commented.

The kind comments on Facebook weren't just received in passing, they meant so much to me. My self-esteem had dipped drastically during the divorce. All the love, even through social media, was restoring. I had also posted a picture from the end of my run—I thought the running skirt and tiara were cute.

"Nice job Melissa, and you look super cute too!" a friend had agreed.

Another friend's mom whom I had met while volunteering at the Ironman race the year before commented, "You look so darling in this picture!"

I also liked to share the fun things I was doing with my kids through social media. Pictures from Zion National Park for example. But occasionally I was now posting more vulnerable insights into our life.

> Had a great night with my kids after being apart for several days. We had fun hanging out and laughing and ended the night with snuggling turned wrestling with the boys. They give me this special feeling in my heart that is just amazing. It's all worth it.

Or I liked to post about new things I was accomplishing. It was surprising how motivating it was to compose a Facebook post in my head while I was doing something hard, a difficult ride or run. Or for other things that popped up.

> It's official. I fixed my first flat on my bike. But that's not good enough, so I did it twice! In lovely Melissa fashion I 'fixed' it the first time with the old tube, haha! But it was great because the second time around I knew what I was doing, and it really is simple. Can't help it, I feel pretty cool now.

> Another one to add to the Single Mom Diaries... replaced my first sprinkler head today. Also fertilized the lawn this morning and got the trimmer started

without any issues. Guess I've been flooding it all this time! It's amazing how much energy you have when you get up at five to run stairs at the track!

It was like journaling, and I knew I would never remember most of these things if I didn't take pictures or write them down. Before the kids had left, I had posted as well.

> Snuggling with my six-year-old Jacob, and he tells me he wants his bedroom to be right next to mine. I explain that there is no bedroom directly next to mine, and he says, 'make your toilet into a room for me.' Haha, I suppose he meant my bathroom. I'm already missing my kids. They are heading with their dad tomorrow. But I will enjoy the time with my hygiene girls this week and family this weekend.

My Uncle Mark, whose home we were swimming at, asked a favor of me. Would I bring some pigeons to a buyer who lived near me? He loved animals and had bred many on his estate— the year before he had given my kids an adorable white rabbit. Apparently, someone wanted his pigeons. Let's just say the ride home was interesting with boxes of pigeons in the back of the van. This minivan had seen all sorts of things.

Back at home, the basement was coming along. I was hoping to have the inspection done by mid-July. Luckily, Flirter Number One was done with his work. I was keeping my distance at this point, and he didn't seem to have hard feelings about it.

I had pulled funds from my savings account for the basement. This meant that I would need to take out a small student loan for the next year of school. It was only around five thousand dollars since I had received multiple scholarship funds. One was from the University for academics, and the other was from the AmeriCorps program for my service in the dental hygiene clinic with underserved populations. After my divorce I had also been eligible for a Pell Grant, but surprisingly all three of these still didn't cover the cost of the program. Thankfully I hadn't needed to get a job. My child support and alimony kept us comfortable and allowed me to focus on school and family.

A couple of the guys I had dated were doing well with other women, even getting married. Tyler of the swoon-worthy voice was dating someone, and it had sounded like it was getting serious. But then he called me venting about her one day. She seemed high maintenance, so I wasn't holding my breath for him. Many guys I'd met tended to be drawn toward attractive, high maintenance, and wild girls. I didn't get it. Sure, that could be fun for a while. I understood that part. But these were guys with kids, and I didn't see how they could justify it. I was looking for the complete package: responsible, fun, and kind. With a healthy amount of chemistry, of course.

In contrast, I was disappointed to hear that Jenny of No Excuses was getting divorced. Even worse was what she had to tell me the next time I saw her.

"Mel, you won't believe it! We haven't even been officially divorced yet and he's seeing someone!" she told me as we pedaled side by side.

"Oh Jenny, how did you find that out? How long has he been seeing her?" I was horrified for her.

"I don't know. I mean he said it was just recent, but he's introduced the kids already!" She had every reason to be upset.

"Wait, how can he—why would he do that?" I was surprised he would take that chance.

"Oh, he's telling the kids we're already divorced. But we're not. I mean we came to terms, but it's not official till the judge stamps it. It hasn't gone through the system yet." She rolled her eyes, emphasizing her disgust with her ex-husband.

I was on her side. It was a dumb move on his part. But also, she had to play it carefully.

"What did you say to your kids?" I asked.

"What am I supposed to say? I told them it wasn't done, but they don't believe me. He's too convincing. If I fight them on it, I'll just make them upset at me."

Unfortunately, she was probably right. It may not be a battle worth fighting, it would be a moot point soon. I tried to change direction of the conversation.

"How are you feeling with him gone, though? Is your day to day better?" I asked.

"Oh, one hundred percent!" she may have exaggerated slightly. "I don't know how I did it for so long. Each day was like walking on eggshells around him and he was controlling about everything."

"Well, that's good then. Keep that in mind. If anything, you should feel bad for the poor girl he's dating now!" We both laughed and I fell behind her as we approached a narrow roadway.

I had heard this before from other women—that their husbands were "controlling" or "narcissists." These were hot topics on social media sites as well. "Five Signs of a Narcissistic Partner" a headline might read, or "Four Steps to Heal Trauma from a Narcissistic Relationship." I wondered if controlling, narcissist husbands were really that commonplace. Or could it be poor communication in a bad marriage being interpreted in a way that created an antagonist and a victim?

However, one woman I knew had been in a truly emotionally abusive marriage. She was a patient that had been assigned to me in the school clinic. As all my interactions with school patients went, we spent many hours together. After hearing that I had been divorced, her story came out gradually over the several appointments we spent together.

Her name was Mandy. She had four children and had shown me pictures of them, exuding the excitement a mother has for her children. Her personality and warmth assured me that she was a good mother. She seemed to care for me as well even though we had only just met. Her kids were older now, but she told me stories of what it was like when they had been younger, and she was still married. Her ex-husband had been a tyrant, but not always obvious to those on the outside. Everything she had done at home was to try and keep the peace, to keep her husband happy. But she'd never been able to tell what would set him off. If she didn't clean the dishes soon enough or listened to music he didn't find appropriate, he could become outraged. Or what she'd found even worse was when he was cold and silent. Then she was nervous, waiting for the explosion. He had never hit her, but he was verbally abusive and demeaning even in front of their children. At times he'd taken out his anger both verbally and physically on the kids, the oldest son in particular. She had withdrawn into herself until she was only a shell of who she had been before her marriage.

She had been rescued in an unexpected way when she discovered her husband was having an affair. He had appeared very remorseful at first and wanted to go to counseling, but he continued to see the other woman. When Mandy confronted him, he'd become defensive and explained that *she* needed him and would even leave their family to go to *her* rescue. Then, other times he had poured out confessions to seemingly relieve himself of the guilt he harbored. Later he'd returned to Mandy to taunt her with visions of this new person he lusted after. To talk about how he wanted to spend his life with *her*—how he could become a better person for *her*. She had allowed it for months until she'd finally gained the self-worth and confidence to give him an ultimatum. He had to leave the other woman and commit to working on their marriage or leave. He left soon after.

Unfortunately, even though he had left her home and was with the other woman, he had wanted to keep the power he'd held over Mandy. He had found ways to use their children as pawns in his game of control. If he had been able to get her alone, he'd lecture her endlessly on all her faults and weaknesses that he had created in his mind. One day she had finally said "No." She wouldn't allow him to talk to her that way anymore. She didn't owe him anything, and what he said didn't align with what others said about her. She made room for positive voices in her head and in her life. She'd slowly moved forward, and by the time I met her I would never have guessed at what she'd been through. She had developed a strength and resilience that was seen even from the outside.

I was blessed to have great examples of strong women around me. My friend Janet was one of those. One afternoon, Janet invited us over to her clubhouse pool. Michael and Olivia had other plans with friends which was just as well. Jake and Crew were the closest of our kids.

"What's your next race?" she asked me as we laid in the sun and the boys played in the pool.

I filled her in with the details of the century ride and 10k swim.

"Wow, those are some big events, that's awesome Melissa!" She led me to the edge of the pool so we could dip our legs.

"I'm trying to be as amazing as you! I wish I had your arms though," I teased though I was completely serious.

Janet was strong and had a naturally toned appearance. A better characteristic still was her heart. When Ezra and I had first decided to separate, Janet was one of the first people I had confided in. She and her husband had been there for me many times. They invited me and the kids over, or even just me when they knew I was by myself and needed company. I appreciated them. Life would be much harder without the good people that surrounded me.

Another one of those good people was Larissa, a friend from when we lived in the Midwest for Ezra's graduate school. She now lived forty-five minutes north of me and we had reconnected recently. I had decided to go up for a visit on a weekend when the kids would be gone. A professional cycling tour would be coming through and I wanted to watch the race. Some friends from the triathlon club were going up as well so that would be fun. Also, this area was known for its annual renaissance festival, and I had plans to go to a play. I had invited someone that I'd met online—Chiropractor, 44—to join me since he lived there, and we hadn't had a chance to go out yet.

As it turned out, Larissa and her husband knew him and teased me about it. They had worked out with him and told me that he was in great shape. But when he arrived at their home, I was a little concerned. I worried that I was taller than him, something that always made me feel uncomfortable. He may have been the same height as me or even slightly taller, but it was hard to tell. Why was this such a big deal? I think I liked feeling like a petite woman in the arms of a taller man. But I wasn't dumb enough to let that stop me from having a good evening and exploring the possibilities. Besides, Chiro, 44 had pulled up in a beautiful classic car. It was a turquoise 1966 Thunderbird convertible with a white top. I had never been in a car like that. The front seat was big, and he gestured for me to sit in the middle near him.

"Come on over, don't make me feel like I'm all alone," he invited.

"You don't have to ask me twice." I laughed and complied easily enough.

His teenage son had been helping him work on the car and they were about finished. He got major points for style. We cruised up a canyon to a popular steakhouse and enjoyed the conversation, going through the usual get to know you and how we had become single.

Unfortunately, I don't think he loved the play. He would probably have been happy to leave at the intermission, but I wanted to see the end. As we cruised through the town afterward, we talked about the families we grew up in and a bit about our faith. I could tell he was a good person. He walked me to the front door of Larissa's home—it was strange being dropped off at someone else's house.

"I had a great time," I started. "That dinner was delicious, and cruising in your beautiful car was nice."

As I stepped forward to give him a hug, he surprised me by moving in for a kiss. One soft one and I started to back up, but he put his arm over my shoulder and pulled me back toward his lips. Two, three, four more? Then he released me to stagger backward.

"I had a great time too. Let's do it again soon," he suggested in a low voice.

I nodded and smiled, still stunned.

Luckily, Larissa and her family were in bed as I crept to the guest room and undressed. That kiss had been unexpected. Chiro, 44 had some chemistry up his sleeve I hadn't been ready for. I had thought he was quite strait-laced, and that moment seemed almost out of character. Honestly, maybe men thought that about me. I was a responsible, no-nonsense person so I could possibly surprise someone with my spontaneous, passionate side. I had better not discount this guy because he was a lot like what I had been looking for.

CHAPTER 8
Drafting

For the century ride in July, I traveled with friends to the even smaller town an hour away that was hosting the event. We settled into a motel and stayed up late prepping our gear. Even with four in the small room, I slept well. Alarms went off early the next morning and we quickly dressed and ate.

The backdrop for the day was incredibly beautiful—red rock was interspersed with swathes of green trees. There would be several stops along the way with food and drinks, which meant we didn't have to carry much with us. In addition to my roomies, we had other friends riding who would help us create a good draft line. We were sticking together and planned to keep a decent pace to finish this thing.

The beginning of any event is always a bit chaotic, and this was no exception. With the large crowd of cyclists moving forward I had to be careful. Sure enough, someone wiped out and took several others with them. I wasn't sure what exactly had happened, I just steered clear.

I thought about the first time I had drafted someone on my bike. It had been a forty-mile ride with No Excuses, and on the way home I was dragging and in danger of getting dropped. Everett had only been out with us a few times since his bike accident and had been keeping his distance, not drafting at all. The day I'd met the group in the hot tub had been one of Everett's first workouts back. He didn't particularly love swimming, but it had taken him even longer to bike with the group again. That wasn't surprising as he'd been life flighted from the scene of his accident. He'd sustained a brain injury that had affected even his personality, months after you'd have thought he was physically recovered. His wife, family and friends had been patient and loving. But it was a huge ordeal. It was understandable he wouldn't want to jump right back into being in a draft line.

So, it had been surprising when Everett had circled back for me and taught me how to draft. He'd invited me to draw close to his back tire and I was worried about it. I was in decent control of my bike at this point, but this was a lot of pressure. He was kind and calm and put me at ease. He had pulled me almost the whole way back and I'd felt the instant relief when I got in the pocket behind his tire. My legs still pedaled at the same cadence, but suddenly the bike moved much faster. We'd caught the group in no time.

As the century crowd thinned, our group pulled together in a draft line. Throughout the day there were about fifteen different cyclists that would come in and out of our line, eight to ten at a time. Usually on big hills we would break up and climb at our own pace. But it turned out to be a windy day and keeping together helped a lot. I took my turn pulling at the front of the line but wasn't the strongest of the group by any stretch, so it was difficult for me to keep up the challenging pace for very long from that position.

There were small stops for water, sports drinks, snacks, and toilets. The largest stop had more considerable food like small sandwiches and chips. Then at the finish there was a full barbeque meal. When I dismounted my bike, I was thankful that I didn't have to run. I really didn't want to do a full Ironman that involved riding a distance even longer than this and doing a marathon afterward. Not to mention starting with a 2.4-mile swim. My rear end was done for the day, but I was feeling better than expected. I hadn't needed to use any special creams for saddle sores like others, but my body would be protesting tomorrow. It was another major milestone—I had biked 106.9 miles in six and a half hours. It was a huge accomplishment for me.

When I opened my eyes Monday morning I was surrounded. Stuffed animals were tucked in front of me as I lay on my side, and I could feel them behind as well. Jake was kneeling on the bed working on balancing them on top of me.

"Hi buddy, come snuggle with me," I invited.

He climbed under the covers, moving a puppy and shark out of the way to make room.

"Oh, pardon me. I meant King Jacob. Do you have any commands for me this morning?"

"Chocolate chip pancakes!" he blurted without too much thought.

Today Jacob was "King for the day" and we had discussed his plans the evening before. They included the arcade and pizza, and I thought we'd probably end up at the pool as well. This had been an idea of my mom's the year before and was back by popular demand. I helped guide their ideas for the itinerary but was impressed they were never too greedy. They usually had a fun activity and favorite food as part of their days. Olivia and Michael would have their turns on other days, Olivia a "Queen" on her day. Their time would have to wait though since they were headed with their dad for the week. At least I had plans too.

My extended family had a ranch in Wyoming, about two hours from where my parents lived. It was a good experience while growing up because we got a taste for the country life. We rode horses, fished, and enjoyed the great outdoors. Because I had lived far away for years, I hadn't spent much time up there with my kids. But I had introduced them to the ranch the year before and they loved it. Jake especially loved being outside with four-wheelers in the summer or snowmobiles in the winter. Michael benefited from having aunts and uncles around that enjoyed the same strategy games he did. And

Olivia had fun with all of it. It was a lengthy drive from our home so we would stay at least three nights when we went. I had planned two trips for July. The kids had come with me for Independence Day and now I was headed back alone.

During the summer and on holidays, there could be thirty or more at the ranch. But there was a lot of space with a big lodge and two smaller cabins. The lodge had four condos inside, and between the condos were large common areas where we could join to eat or play games. Occasionally we even pushed all the furniture back to have a dance night. When the family was gathered, we would usually work on a service project at some point. The projects could vary from moving rocks out of fields to make it possible to plant hay, irrigation or fencing repairs, organizing and cleaning the barn, or any other number of things. On holidays we usually did fireworks—Wyoming was known for being able to get more powerful fireworks legally than in most other states.

Although I drove up alone, I was expecting Jim to join me. His airplane was a small backcountry one with big tires that could land easily on dirt roads, and he was excited to fly in. When my family found out what was happening, they all got excited as well. By time Jim flew in there was a group of at least twenty-five lining the wooden fence next to the dirt road. He had our location's coordinates, and we found a large flag to identify the beginning of our property for him. There were whoops and hollers when he was spotted followed by a big cheer as he made a safe and smooth landing. After he taxied over, some of the bigger kids gathered rocks to put under the large tires. He let the smaller cousins get inside the plane to see what it looked like. It was an event for the whole family!

I started getting questions about Jim. I shrugged them all off, we were just friends. They didn't believe me or didn't want to because they all thought he was so cool. Uncle Mark was especially curious and pulled me aside when Jim was out of earshot.

"Tell me about this guy Melissa. What's his story, are you guys getting serious?"

"We spend a lot of time together and I like him a lot, but I don't think a long-term relationship would work with Jim," I confided.

"Why is that? Is he a good guy?" he prodded.

"Yeah, he is. But I don't know if we have the same outlook on life and I have to consider my kids too," I answered.

"I get it, that's good. I'm glad you're thinking that all through." He smiled and gave me a side squeeze, dropping the interrogation.

Naturally the next morning Jim and I went for a run out to the old pioneer schoolhouse on the property. It was hard enough for me to run with Jim at two thousand feet elevation so it was a task indeed at over eight thousand feet. He took me and my dad up in the Cessna later in the morning. It was a great opportunity for my dad to get pictures of the ranch from above, he'd never had this perspective before. I had a much better flight than the last time Jim had taken me out. On the last trip he had flown over a plateau and followed the cliff down (straight down it felt like) before pulling back up and leveling off. My stomach had turned inside out, and I got clammy like I was going to pass out. He did a similar move off the mountain bench across from the ranch. Either I was ready for it this time, or it wasn't as drastic because it didn't bother me as much.

Jim took off that evening and he had another crowd lined up along the fence cheering him on. He obliged us by doing a fly-by once he was up in the air. Uncle Mark threw his arms in the air and the kids squealed. Too bad we weren't a true match because the family had fallen in love with him!

The next week Michael was gone to a youth camp, and I tried to keep the other two entertained that week as well. We went to the movies, pool, shopping mall, basically anywhere that would keep us cool. We picked up Michael on Friday and the kids were with me over the weekend. Chiropractor, 44 really wanted to see me so he came down and took me to lunch on Saturday. It was nice to have some more time to chat and be around each other.

Occasionally I would sneak in a short date when the kids were with me. I would meet at the location instead of being picked up, so they weren't meeting every guy. Michael was already unhappy about those that he *had* met. He'd told me that he didn't want to get to know someone if they weren't going to stick around.

In contrast to Michael, Olivia wanted details about everyone! When the divorce was almost official, she had been extremely upset and even nervous at the prospect of me dating. But we'd had a good heart-to-heart about it. She had been particularly focused on having a stepdad. I'd told her to think of all the cool guys she knew, mainly my brothers and brothers-in-law. She loved all of them and they weren't scary. I'd explained that when I got married again someday, it would only be to an amazing man that she would love too. After that chat she had been super excited about the whole thing. Jake didn't seem to care at all, as if he wasn't even aware of it.

This was also an exciting week as the home inspector was scheduled to come do his final walkthrough. It would be such a relief have this done. At first it had seemed like an insurmountable task, but here we were at the finish line! I didn't have any reason to believe we wouldn't pass inspection. The inspector had been there at different stages along the way, and I was confident we had followed all his instructions. Sure enough, he gave the thumbs up. The sense of accomplishment easily matched how I had felt when I finished my century ride, half marathon, or any of the triathlons. I think the kids were as excited as I was, as they should be. We had doubled the size of our home!

The next weekend was a major event—the 10K swim marathon. This is something I had been looking forward to for months. The triathlon club president Travis had been working with me at the reservoir during our weekly Wednesday evening swims. Travis had taught me how to draft, just as Everett had taught me on the bike. When he'd found out about my 10K swim he brought it up, I had never heard of such a thing for swimming. But sure enough, as I'd neared his feet and stayed in his path of bubbles, I'd been able to keep the same speed without as much effort. A couple of times we'd played a cat and mouse game. We would take turns in front working hard, then at some point the "cat" would overtake the "mouse" from behind and become the leader. It increased the overall pace and those were my fastest swims ever.

For the trip, I towed my tent trailer behind the minivan. It was truly a tent on a trailer; nothing fancy but comfortable and easy to set up. Inside were two full-sized beds and a table came down between them. Jim and I tied the kayak down on top of the trailer. The plan was to camp the night before the race, I didn't worry about Jim and I sharing the tent. We weren't involved physically and with a race he was even more strict than me about getting to bed early. We went to see where the race would be and did a short swim to stretch out my muscles. Then we ate at a nearby café and were asleep not long after dark.

The day started out cool. Luckily, I would be swimming in a full wetsuit. We had protein shakes and bars ready for breakfast. Jim had all the magic powders and gels ready for the swim. He would tell me what to take and when, I trusted him with all my nutrition decisions. Besides, it made it easier for me to focus on the swim. The water was a bit of a shock to my feet, but I knew it would all pass within moments after the start. Jim had the kayak in the water ready to go.

My main purpose at the start of the swim was to find an individual or small group as the crowd dissipated and I could get my bearings. Travis had instructed me to find someone who was keeping my pace, get on their feet, and follow their bubbles. As the horn blared, I dove in and got to work, my face quickly getting used to the cold. It wasn't the same frenzy I was used to in triathlons. There was a much smaller crowd with several hanging back intentionally. We all knew we would be doing this for a while. Most were entered in the 5K swim, less in the full 10K.

We curved around the first buoy and followed the shoreline to the right. I could see Jim off to my left. Before long the swimmers started to separate, and I noticed two swimmers on my right that were swimming in tandem at my same pace. I cut over and got right behind the second swimmer. The pace was brisk, I had trained enough that I could keep up a quicker turnover with my arms and not fatigue. Endurance was one thing, but Travis had helped me get to a place where I could have both distance *and* speed. The first ten to fifteen minutes was still a warm-up, but after that it got easier. There was something freeing about swimming in open water without lane ropes or walls necessitating flip turns. There were times when it seemed like I could go forever. Today I would be testing my limits.

I didn't pay much attention, but our three kayak supporters must have been communicating with each other. They circled the wagons, so to speak, and we popped our heads out of the water.

"Hey guys, I hope you don't mind that I joined you. I'm more than happy to take my turn pulling. Would you like me to go next?" I asked between breaths.

The first swimmer was a woman in her mid to late twenties wearing a sleeveless wetsuit. The second was a middle-aged man in a mere Speedo. Without expending too much energy they both gave their approval. Jim handed me a bottle with some kind of electrolyte concoction inside which he forced me to finish even though I resisted. He also made me choke down a gel and collected my trash. We didn't hang on the kayaks, just tread water next to them. After maybe five minutes tops we were off with me taking the lead.

There was a tangible difference being in the front doing the pulling. I had to kick harder and turn my arms over even faster to keep the same pace. I wanted to make sure I was never holding them back and was motivated to do my part. It must have been at least forty-five minutes in this formation so when we stopped, I was ready for it. This time I floated on my back as we took a break next to the support kayaks. My muscles were starting to tighten across my shoulder blades and all the way down my back. I gulped down everything Jim handed me knowing I couldn't afford to shirk on nutrition. We were getting closer but had at least another forty-five minutes, maybe more. This would require me to dig deep.

I took my place between the other two swimmers as we built our pace back up. The first fifteen to twenty minutes after the break weren't too bad, but then everything started getting progressively worse. My back was screaming, and I wondered if I would've taken another break if I didn't have swimmers in front and behind me forcing me to continue.

I am strong, I am strong – I was repeating in my mind. Swimming was a lonely sport and I almost always had something running through my mind on a constant loop. Often it was the last song I had heard, or sometimes I would use the time to go over memorized scriptures or schoolwork. At this moment, I was creating my own positive mantras to keep me focused and engaged. I was envisioning how I looked in the water and how it would feel swimming up to the finish buoy.

My mind wandered to my first open water swim. Two friends had been my support that day, but on paddle boards. They paddled alongside me as I ventured out into the reservoir, making sure I was safe. The distance that day had probably been one thousand meters and I'd considered it a big accomplishment. Here I was, completing *ten* thousand meters. Being reminded of how far I had come in the last couple of years supplied me with the drive to keep my arms going and push through the pain.

As we rounded the corner and I could see the finish buoy near the boat ramp where we had started, a major adrenaline rush kicked in. The same must have happened for the other two. Suddenly our feet were kicking hard above the water, and our pace picked up in a way I hadn't thought was possible with how I had been feeling. We sprinted to the buoy, and each touched it signifying our completion of the race. As our kayakers circled in, we swimmers hugged each other and tried to catch our breath. I was on an incredible high. Pictures were taken then we floated on our backs and stretched them out. There wasn't another group near us so we could soak in the moment.

Eventually we made our way out of the water and said our goodbyes. We'd made quick introductions in the water and could find each other on Facebook. Jim helped unzip my wetsuit and I peeled it off my shoulders. The high was starting to come down and was quickly being replaced by pain. I was given a finisher medal and we took more pictures. All I could think now was how badly I needed to get some ibuprofen in my system. Immediately. I didn't know how I was even going to sit upright in the car for the ride home. Jim did all the work of strapping the kayak onto the trailer while I found the pills and got them down. I took for granted the fact that he had also paddled the whole way with me. We had finished the swim in two hours and fifty-seven minutes which was a good thirty minutes faster than I had dared hope for.

I talked with Jim as the pain medicine was getting on board, going over the details and reliving the glory. It had been a good experience for both of us and he was proud of me. We grabbed food and kept on driving. Once the pain in my back started dulling, I sacked out. I was so grateful that Jim had the wheel. It was nice to have someone else drive for once—being single meant I was always driving.

The trip home was about four hours, so we arrived by late afternoon. Jim headed home in his own vehicle once we got to my house, and I got straight in the bathtub. The hot water was therapeutic, and I didn't plan to be out for a long while. I settled in with my phone to post my victory on Facebook and catch up on messages.

There was a new message on one of the dating websites.

INBOX:

Triathlons... That's impressive. How long are the run and bike ride that you have to do? My little sister does triathlons. I've never tried anything long distance.

Do you work for a dentist now while you're going to school? My best friend when I was growing up there is now a dentist. How much schooling do you have left?

What are some of the spontaneous things you've done with your kids that have been fun? I'm supposed to be going camping with my girls next weekend.

I look forward to hearing back from you.

What a good message. He had taken the time to read through my profile and say some nice things. So many of the messages I got were completely shallow and devoid of intelligence. This deserved a response.

SENT:

Hi! I have been doing triathlons about a year and a half now and it has been great motivation and a fun way to meet new people. After divorce I really needed to get out and have a social life! Distances... it depends. The biggest triathlon I've done is the Ironman 70.3 which is 1.2 swim, 56 bike and 13.1 run. Just finished a big swim race today. 10k or 6.2 miles...it was awesome!

I have one year left in school. I don't work *for* a dentist but *with* some in our school clinic.

Our summer has been busy, but I took them camping last summer and had a great time. I like to take them to the pool when we can or anything else that strikes our fancy :)

What do you do for work?

INBOX:

I would need floaties to be able to finish 10k in the water. How many people did you compete against? Were you happy with how you finished?

I work for a large electrical contractor in Las Vegas. I'm on the preconstruction side which means I'm in charge of sales, estimating, and I help with designing the electrical and lighting for new buildings. I've been doing it for about eighteen years. It's a fast-paced job.

So, what have been your favorite vacation spots? Or where is your dream vacation spot?

SENT:

There were maybe twenty who competed in my particular distance. As you can imagine, not many want to do this kind of race. I actually came in thirty minutes before I had dared hope, so I am very happy.

I finished my basement recently so I learned a few things and can appreciate how busy you must get.

Favorite vacation spots ever? Off the top of my head, I am thinking Lake Powell and Europe. I have never been on a cruise or anywhere tropical, so that is next on my list! What about you?

INBOX:

In the last house I built we had a basement. I built a theater room in it that I loved.

Lake Powell is awesome. I certified in scuba diving when I was fourteen at Lake Powell. Where did you go in Europe? I would love to visit and see some of the sites. Not sure if I would like southern France more or to just see some of the WWII sites. I love history.

Most of my vacations have been to the beach. Florida beaches aren't too impressive. Mexico before all of the violence used to be one of my favorite places. Cancun is better than the Bahamas or Hawaii as far as beaches are concerned. The sand is like Bisquik. It's been a few years since I've been there, and I would love to go back except now I would go a little south of Cancun. My idea of a great vacation is deciding whether to hang out at the pool or the beach, minimal luggage (swimsuits don't take too much space), and good local food. I also have a bunch of places here in the states I would love to visit.

How long did you swim for?

SENT:

I have a very small theater room downstairs, but I still need to buy all the equipment. I think it will be awesome!

I have been to beaches in Cali, Florida and Italy but Cancun sounds exactly like what I am looking for. Though if I can, I will head to Puerto Rico in the next year because my sister is living there. I did a study abroad in Germany and also traveled through Switzerland, Italy, and Prague.

I am totally with you on good local food. I have cities I remember based on meals I ate there, haha! I am all about good food :)

My time was 2:57... then I drove home and got in the bath for an hour. Hahaha!

So, what did you do so far this weekend? What do you like to do with your downtime?

We continued back-and-forth for a few more messages before winding down. I learned he liked to do CrossFit, in fact he sounded about as obsessed with it as I was with triathlon. We discovered we had a favorite restaurant in common, my Monday usual Thai place! But it was time to get out of the bathtub. I could message CrossFit, 42 some more tomorrow.

CHAPTER 9
Injured, not Broken

Church without the kids again this week. I was teaching the ages twelve to thirteen Sunday school class. When Ezra and I were first separated, I'd struggled to keep up as president of the children's organization and had eventually asked to be replaced. For the past year I'd had the perfect job for me; I'd led the music in the women's class. It hadn't taken much preparation time at all, and I enjoyed doing it. Teaching the twelve to thirteen-year-olds was new and going well. It was a good challenge to get them to participate and absorb at least a little something throughout the forty-five-minute lesson time. Some had moved up from the children's group recently, so I knew them and how to engage their interest better.

The long, lonely Sunday afternoon didn't seem as bad today. I was pretty worn out from the day before and needed rest. Besides, I had someone new to chat with and messaged a bit with CrossFit, 42. We picked up where we had left off, this time learning more about our kids and situations. For example, I learned that his son was preparing to serve as a missionary as he had. It was a good sign for me that faith was a foundation in his life.

INBOX:

Your kids start school tomorrow? Mine don't go back for a couple of weeks. Austin just graduated as you saw in the photo on my profile. He is working until he gets his mission assignment. He's a great kid. Claire turns fifteen in November, and she starts HS this year. She is really smart and doesn't settle. She's always doing her homework even if she has to get up at five a.m. Ivy is the fun-loving girly girl. She just turned ten. She is good at school but even better at socializing and looking fabulous. I don't think she has ever had a bad day. She is my sunshine.

Sometimes knowing how to build things can be a curse. I need a chest of drawers for my bedroom and can't find exactly what I need so I am probably going to make it myself. The plus is I get exactly what I want the downside is it takes time.

How many classes do you have this fall?

Do you share custody with your ex? Does he live near you?

SENT:

My oldest, Michael, is turning fifteen in January. He really loves his technology, but also works out with his dad in the mornings and is a black belt in karate. Olivia is eleven and a fun combination of tomboy and girly girl. Also a black belt who now loves to dance. Jacob is turning seven next month but looks a couple of years older easily. He is so tall! But still loves to snuggle his mama.

I understand the blessing and curse of knowing how to do things. I lived in a half-finished house for many years cause my ex was going to do it but wasn't terribly motivated after working long days. I'm sure you feel the same way.

My school schedule is pretty busy. Full time, not sure about this semester but usually around twenty credit hours. They own us, we don't even register ourselves. We don't have options, just have to be there. Three days a week I am there eight to five. My kids are good about helping with meals and being on their own a bit after school.

Their dad is in town and has the kids two days a week. Joint custody, but not half and half per se. What is your arrangement like?

INBOX:

I just picked up my girls. We have them equal time. She has them one week and then I have them one week. We exchange the girls on Sunday nights. I get them this whole next week. I love hanging out and talking to them. Your kids are similar in ages except for the youngest. That's pretty cool they do martial arts. I'm sure it's good for the self-esteem.

When I built my house there were definitely some projects I took on because I had to not that I wanted to. Like the stair railings. Not a fun project but I saved about $4k. That was a couple of really late nights.

Your schedule is going to be packed. That's a lot of class time not including any homework. When I was in high school, I played all three sports and worked until midnight almost every night. No time for homework. I used to do homework in between classes. It worked okay except for calculus. I think

I actually did more algebra homework for my girlfriend than my own homework. Funny thing is her algebra teacher was my uncle. Halfway through the year he told me how impressed he was with my algebra skills.

Your family seems driven. You swimming across the ocean and a bunch of superhero black belt kids. It's quite impressive. Do your kids do other sports?

SENT:

Yeah, we all sound good on paper, but I feel like we have been pretty lazy this summer. We haven't done a whole lot of sports with them, maybe it's because I have always been into individual sports and my ex didn't really do sports in high school either.

I was lucky in high school. I didn't have a job except for working for my dad. I was involved in high school clubs and the swim team of course. I can't imagine working until midnight and keeping up with everything. Talk about driven!

If you would like to text me sometime, feel free. I am not always very regular at checking my messages on here.

Have a good night!

INBOX:

I will give you a call this week maybe we could find a good local place up by you to have dinner. Good night. Good luck with the first day of school!

The first day of school went well. I managed to get pictures of Olivia and Jake, but Michael was getting old for that, so I didn't push him. I had two weeks until my classes started and intended to make the most of it in the meantime. That week I returned the kayak, got a massage, had lunch with a girlfriend, and went to an orientation for the fall semester. I did some longer rides and runs as well to be better prepared for the 70.3 triathlon I was doing soon. We went up to visit with my family over the weekend. I loved being closer to them and wanted my kids to get more time with their grandparents, aunts, uncles, and cousins after years of living far away.

Later in the week CrossFit, 42 gave me an old-fashioned call on the phone. At times I had messaged with a guy, and when I finally met him in person his voice didn't match what I'd imagined in my head. That could be weird. So, the best part about this call was that I got to hear CrossFit, 42's voice. I liked it. It was low and gravelly, a real man's voice.

I enjoyed talking with you for a bit this evening. So, I have a question for you...

I just finished my workout. What's your question? Feel free to call if it's more than a yes/no question.

Nice! I'm just curious about your current facial hair status...you have pics with and without a beard ☺

Haha. That's funny. Hard to explain in a text. It was my "protest beard". I started it this last Christmas. I have never had facial hair before. Is that bad?

Hahaha, and I cut my hair short

I don't think it's bad, I was just curious

Wait, how long have you been divorced? Protest?

I realized when I was on vacation that I didn't need to shave because I was home, my then wife obviously didn't care and I wasn't trying to impress anybody else so I just let it go. I've been divorced for 2-1/2 months. I haven't shaved it all the way off yet. Just trimmed shorter now.

Did the 2-1/2 month thing scare you off?

Wow! No, I know I personally felt ready to date the minute my ex walked out the door honestly ;)

There are times it still feels pretty new to me and it has been a year! Just time.

Sunday the kids headed back to their dad's, and I went alone to the church ice cream social. I didn't want to stay too long, I was planning on a phone call from CrossFit, 42 to arrange a dinner date for tomorrow evening. Not surprisingly, when he called, we decided on our favorite Thai restaurant. I laughed, thinking everyone that worked there would be proud of me for having a date!

The next morning, I did a bike and run with No Excuses. In the afternoon Jim had scheduled reflexology appointments for us. My feet had been sore trying to build up my miles. I would be running 13.1 miles this Saturday and needed all the help I could get. Reflexology massages were interesting because you stayed fully clothed, and they massaged right over top. It was very relaxing, therapeutic, and the bonus was that it cost less than my normal masseuse.

When CrossFit, 42 picked me up at my house for our dinner date I was surprised by his appearance at the doorstep.

"Wait, where's your beard?" I asked him.

"I shaved it off since you don't like beards." He shrugged as we headed to the driveway.

"Hey, I never said that!" I shook my head and and knitted my eyebrows.

Really? He had done that for me, and we hadn't even met before? He had also driven two hours from work and looked nice in a pair of slim work slacks and short-sleeved button-down shirt. As he opened the car door for me, I noticed that it was immaculate. But what impressed me even more was the music he was playing.

"Is this the music you like to listen to?" I asked sounding strangely suspicious.

"Yeah…is that okay?"

I laughed. "Of course, I guess I was just surprised. This is exactly the stuff I listen to. I love alternative."

We discussed our favorite bands and songs and before long were at the restaurant. I ordered the panang curry, of course, and he ordered the same. Seated next to a saltwater fish tank, he was excited to point out some details since he had a tank himself. We talked about our formative high school years and families. He had grown up across town from where I now lived, and his parents were still in the same house.

Conversation was going well, and he asked for dessert recommendations. I told him about a cupcake place that was yummy and had different flavors each day. We swung by and picked some up then took them back to my house. Sitting at the kitchen table, we ate the cupcakes and continued talking. We were laughing pretty good at one point and got along easily. After walking him to the front door at the end of the evening, I gave him a hug and may have startled him a bit. I had to remember he was new to this. In fact, I think I may have been his first date.

Since it was the last week before my classes started, I had a few projects to do. The shutters were installed in the basement, then I got my hair done and took the minivan to get serviced. On Friday, I drove north for the triathlon and stayed at my sister Leah's again. I met Jim and friends at an Italian restaurant for the traditional carb-loading dinner. But we didn't stay late so I got a chance to spend some time with Leah and her kids before I went to bed early.

The weather forecast wasn't looking good. We had been watching it for days and I still wasn't sure what to expect. In the morning the darkness was so thick it seemed the sun would never come up. As I arrived at the lake where the swim would be, I only felt worse. Athletes were huddled in their vehicles as sprinkling rain turned to steady rain turned to an all-out downpour! Flashes of lightning streaked the sky which not only struck me with fear, but disappointment as well. They wouldn't let us race if this didn't clear up, and fast. It would be such a sad waste to be here and only get to do a part of the race if they canceled the swim portion. Contrarily, the lightning somehow invoked laughter from me each time it struck. Some athletes had not been quick enough at retrieving their gear from the transition area and now their socks and shoes were soaked. Our poor bikes were drenched as well, and the puddles were so large I was getting worried for the ride and the road conditions.

Miraculously, after about an hour the skies cleared providing the most perfect race weather ever. August could have meant extreme heat, so the rain proved to be a blessing in disguise. The cool morning made for an uncomfortable swim start, but the cold didn't compare to what I had in store when I put my face in the water. Nothing. Pitch black nothingness. I was shocked, I'd never had this experience. It was literally lights out when I looked under the dark, brown water. It didn't make me feel better knowing I would surely swallow some at some point during the 1.2-mile swim. And there was one more treat in store. The water was shallow enough that people were literally standing up at various points during the entire swim. This was the worst swim course I'd experienced, including the one in the ocean. Not surprisingly, it turned out to be my slowest time as well.

Transitioning to my soaked bike wasn't too bad, but I did have lots of puddles to avoid at first. After that the rainfall had mostly drained from the roads and the ride would've been ideal except there was not one porta potty on the entire bike course. Triathletes are known to relieve themselves right on their bike, but I was definitely not at that level, so I had to find a secluded patch of tall grass to squat. Many weren't even bothering to hide—it was turning out to be quite the adventure!

I must have looked like a newborn foal finding its legs as I started the run. After my muscles loosened up, I had a few good miles, but then I noticed my right foot bothering me. *Don't be a baby,* I thought. *Tough it out, that's what you're here for.* But eventually, I had to take a break and walk. I noticed a woman, maybe in her twenties, walking nearby. We exchanged some complaints from the day so far and were soon in conversation. In fact, we ended up finishing the half marathon together. We would walk for a time, then pick a point where we would start running again. After several minutes, we would choose a new landmark to go back to walking. Alternating this way got us through it, but when I crossed the finish line I was spent. Even with the walking I had shaved forty minutes off from the Oceanside Ironman 70.3 earlier in the year.

Jim's brother Brody was there watching for all of us as we crossed. Obviously, Jim had finished well before me. Brody told me to lay down and helped stretch out my legs. It was amazing how good it felt to have someone else do that. We found each other and took pictures together before collecting all our gear, which I did with a prominent limp. Jim asked about it, and I said my foot was hurting but I was sure it would go away with the usual soreness in a few days. But just to add a little extra spice to the day, I was stung on the back of my leg by a bee as I walked away with my gear. Wow, really? I was done.

My parents had driven the hour from their home to see me and we met at an Indian buffet. We took pictures to commemorate the day, and I proudly smiled with my finisher tee on and the medal still around my neck. When I got back to Leah's she prepared a foot soak for me accompanied by chocolate cake which made everything better. I limped around and even had a difficult time driving home the next day. Pressing the gas and brake with my right foot in pain was not fun. CrossFit, 42 checked in with me after the race along with Chiro, 44 and even Alaska, 48 who had noticed my Facebook post.

You would think the first week of school would be easy. But with the dental hygiene program, we jumped right back in. I noticed as the days went on my foot was feeling worse and not better, so I finally scheduled an appointment with a podiatrist. The doctor believed I had a stress fracture. He wrapped my foot and scheduled me for an MRI the next week. In the meantime, he put me in a walking boot. Over the weekend the kids were gone for Labor Day with their dad, so I sat at home not doing much of anything.

On Monday, I went to the gym to at least work my arms and abs and swim since I didn't have classes and I figured I couldn't hurt much that way. I did discover that pushing off the pool wall was painful, and I had to be careful. After swimming for a while, I climbed out of the pool to lay in the sun. I happened to be brave that day and was wearing my bikini. Out of the corner of my eye I saw a man in the pool notice me. I laid on the lounge chair and closed my eyes, trying to ignore the feeling of being watched. Eventually I was hot enough that I needed to get back in the pool. When I did, he was waiting.

"You're a good swimmer," he commented. He must have been watching *before* I got out of the pool.

"Thanks," I said shyly.

"Do you swim here all the time?" he asked.

STRENGTH ON THE WATER

"Yes, but usually in the early mornings. And I swim at the reservoir more in the summer, too," I explained.

He seemed surprised. "That's brave! Do you compete or something?"

"Yeah, I like to do triathlons. Just got into it the last couple of years," I answered simply. Sometimes I was embarrassed to talk about triathlon, like I was bragging.

He asked me some more light questions before getting to the personal ones.

"So, are you married? Do you have kids?" Here it came.

"No and yes. Not married and three kids," I answered. "They're with their dad this weekend, so I'm relaxing while I can."

"That's good, you deserve it," he declared. "Do you work?"

"Not right now. I'm in my second year of the dental hygiene program," I told him. He perked up at this. It turned out he was friends with one of my instructors. This was getting weird.

I was surprised, but kind of relieved when he didn't ask for my phone number. That was always a bit awkward.

When I got home, I texted CrossFit, 42.

> I wanted you to know I managed arms and abs just fine today ☺ Oh, and I may also have tried some laps and flip turns while I was laying out at the pool...

> Sounds like you're having a great day. I'm almost jealous.

> Almost? What do I need to do to get you there? Get some Thai takeout?

Hahaha. Ok that would work. Actually, you had me at abs and arms. As soon as it cools down this evening I'm going to work out.

That's right you missed your fix last night, huh? I'm addicted, but you have it way worse than me.

Oh…I'm fully aware that I have a problem. Every night around 7:30 I start getting antsy. My friends tease me that once I start dating that will change.

Maybe, or it could get worse. Depends on a few factors.

What factors? Please tell me. I could always use a little guidance.

I don't know, that's getting kinda personal. For me, working out helps somewhat in my extra energy department…but only somewhat. Being around someone you're really attracted to and not satisfying that can make it worse as far as I'm concerned.

This sounds like a story you need to tell me.

It's not a story. Just facts. Facts of life ;)

Then I went out for Thai because it was Monday and sent a picture to tease him. Our dialogue was getting interesting. I was starting to look forward to our next date more and more. We were set to go out this coming Saturday. The kids would be gone again, one of the rare times they'd be gone three weekends in a row because of the holiday.

My instructor Ms. Thomas approached me the next day to talk about the guy I had met at the pool. He had gotten in touch and asked her all about me. She had said nice things, we were friends to a degree. Her daughter had earned her black belt through the same karate studio as my kids. I was nervous to get too involved with someone that was her friend, but he seemed like a nice enough guy, so I told her she could give him my phone number.

And the conversation with CrossFit, 42 just kept getting better.

> Day 4 of the boot and I am restless already. Not a good sign!

Day 38 is really going to be fun.

> Wow that cheered me up immensely ☺

Haha. Sorry I was going for sympathy.

> And couldn't quite make it?

Hahaha. You got me. I can't even come up with any good comeback right now.

> Uh oh, your numbers are going up on the jerk scale...

I guess I'm going to have to proofread my texts more carefully before hitting the send button. After meeting you the first time I didn't expect you to be one to keep me on my toes like I now know will be required to do (that's a good thing)

Well you can't really get to know someone on the first date. Guess we need a second ;)

I had sent CrossFit, 42 a picture of me in my walking boot so I demanded he reciprocate:

By the way, you owe me a selfie. You can pay up today or tomorrow. Or both.

I don't think I've ever taken a selfie.

You are dating in a new world my friend. Giddy up!

He obeyed and sent one not long after. It was good for a first attempt; guys could be terrible at selfies.

I had the MRI later that week, and it was awful. I had underestimated how difficult and uncomfortable it would be to hold still for that long. The results were back the following afternoon and I got permission to leave early from school. There was good news and bad news. The good news was that I didn't have the stress fracture the doctor had believed was there. The bad news was that I had tendonitis in the same area. I felt like a big baby for spending all the money on the MRI and now he said I needed physical therapy.

Chiro, 44 had invited me to *The Little Mermaid* at the outdoor amphitheater. I was honest and told him I had season tickets and would be taking the kids at the end of the month. But he said if I was okay to see it twice, he would like to take me. He even had the VIP tickets that included dinner before. He drove a more practical vehicle this time, and after eating we sat on the grass to talk a while before going to find our seats.

"Melissa, I need to tell you something."

This sounded ominous. "Okay, what's up?" I tried to sound light.

He cleared his throat. "I told you about my ex-wife before, my kids' mom…"

I nodded, encouraging him to continue.

"Well, I was actually married again after our divorce. I've been married twice." He looked up at me to see my reaction.

I took in a long breath. "Wow, I'm glad you were comfortable enough to share that with me. Tell me about your second wife," I invited.

He shared how they had met not long after his divorce and he'd wanted so badly not to be alone. She was beautiful with a fun personality, and he had jumped in with both feet. Not long after they'd married things had gone downhill. She was never happy and always wanted more from him. She'd started hiding things and taking money from his accounts. Before long she'd also racked up a large amount of debt. The marriage had lasted less than a year.

"Listen, this is hard stuff. I understand. I know how vulnerable I was after my divorce. I'm sorry you had to go through this," I empathized.

I wanted him to know I didn't think less of him and that I was grateful for his honesty. But had it changed how I saw him? I wasn't sure. He held my hand through the show, gripping tightly. I think opening up had made him feel closer to me.

After the show finished, he drove me home and followed me inside the house. We stood by the front door, and I thanked him for the lovely evening. He put his hands on my waist and pushed me against the closed door, kissing me firmly. He moved one hand from my waist and placed it on the door to the side of my face. There was a lot of emotion being poured into that kiss from him and I could feel it.

"I need to go." He stopped the kiss abruptly and backed up.

"You have a long drive," I agreed and reached for the door handle.

He caught my hand and pulled me back toward him. "One more until I can see you again." He kissed me softly this time then opened the door and walked out.

I was disoriented. It was an impressive kiss and I liked him a lot. But I didn't think I was feeling what he was. I had been caught in this situation before. I was a good listener and tried to empathize and help. By nature, this brought me closer to someone and they were drawn to me. But that didn't necessarily mean we were supposed to be together. I hadn't had enough time with him or felt anything to assure me that I should be with him. I needed some sleep.

CHAPTER 10

Time

The next morning, I slept in since I couldn't do much anyway with my foot in pain. Then I took a luxurious shower. The hot water poured over me as I sat on the tile floor of the shower and thought about the night before. I was feeling unsure about that whole situation and was worn out from the late night. Eventually I got up and turned off the shower, wrapping my hair in a towel and putting on a terrycloth robe. Lounging on my bed, I checked my social media and then my school schedule to see what homework needed to be done. I'd try to put in a good couple of hours of work before my date with CrossFit, 42.

We had talked on the phone earlier to coordinate our plans. He would pick me up in the early afternoon for an excursion to the reservoir. I was testing him. Things had been going so well with our conversations that I wanted to see if we had more in common. Being outside and in the water was something I really enjoyed. He'd acted like he was game with the idea when we'd discussed options, so I was eager to see if he'd genuinely have fun out there or if he had just been telling me what I wanted to hear.

When he arrived at my house, he was dressed quite differently from our last date. He looked like he had just walked off the beach in his faded Converse shoes. In fact, his green shirt said "Surf La Jolla" across it. He came bearing gifts—baggies of fresh, sliced peaches he had promised me earlier when he was making peach cobbler. I put them in the freezer, thinking what a great peach milkshake they would make. I showed him to the kids' bathroom so he could change and went to my bedroom to do the same. We met back in the family room, ready to go. Conversation was easy and natural after two and a half weeks of texts and phone calls. I showed him the new backroad to the reservoir, it was a favorite to ride on my bike. We parked near the area that was sectioned off to keep swimmers safe from boats.

"We could swim out to those rocks and do some cliff diving. What do you think?" I pointed out a cluster of red rocks about a hundred yards from the beach.

"Are you serious? Those rocks out there? My idea of swimming is when you have to get back to the boat after you fall waterskiing."

I laughed. Surely, he was just stroking my ego. I took off my shorts and t-shirt, resting them on a rock.

"Well, you'll have to help me with some sunblock, or I'll get fried," he said as he pulled off his shirt as well.

He handed me the bottle and suddenly this seemed so intimate. I had only ever touched him once during our hug, and now I was going to rub my hands all down his shoulders and back.

"You bet!" I exuded confidence though I was nervous as I felt his muscles beneath my fingertips. I fanned the sunblock over his shoulders then down to his lower back. "I think you should be good now," I managed as I handed him back the bottle. I gingerly made my way to the water, babying my foot and waving away any concern CrossFit had.

He continued in his complaint, "Seriously, I hope you've taken lifeguard classes or something, just in case."

We waded out to our knees, and I was starting to question if he really did feel uncomfortable with that distance. But as we took our time leisurely swimming toward the rocks, he didn't seem to struggle. Conversation started up again once we put our feet down.

"Good job, you made it!" I congratulated him with a smirk. "So did you used to waterski a lot then?"

"About every week in the summer. My friend's parents had a boat, and we would take it out all the time," he answered as we started to climb up the red rocks.

We talked more about watersports and boating as we climbed. I had grown up in an avid boating family. We checked out the different options for jumping. I wasn't gutsy enough to go too high. CrossFit started to turn around as if he would do a back flip.

"What are you doing?" I questioned him in surprise.

"A back flip," he answered simply.

"What, are you sure? Is there enough room? I'm worried you'll hit the rock!" I was suddenly very concerned.

He slowly turned around while laughing. "I won't do it if it scares you." Then he jumped off and let out a yell.

I waited till his head bobbed up then pushed off the rock in the other direction so I wouldn't land too close to him. We scrambled up again. This time I didn't go up as high and opted for a dive instead of a jump. From the water I had a perfect vantage point to watch as he finished his climb. I was enjoying the view when he looked down and found me staring at him. Luckily it made sense that I would be watching. He turned around and before I had a chance to protest, he did a perfect back flip and landed not far from me. My heart fluttered a little, this guy was cool.

When he surfaced, I balked, "Hey I thought you weren't going to do a backflip!" Then I swatted the water sending a splash his way. Before he could get me back, I swam quickly back to the rock.

We both jumped a few more times before heading back to shore. After toweling off at the car he drove us back to my house. We cleaned up, he in the kids' bathroom and me in mine. I strapped back on the walking boot I had ditched for the reservoir. We found a light snack at home before heading to a sci-fi movie. We shared a large tub of popcorn, otherwise keeping to ourselves in our own

MELISSA J DELLACA -

seats. But after the movie as we sat on the couch back at home and talked, CrossFit, 42 broke the barrier.

"Give me your hand." He took my hand in his. "Interesting fun fact about me," he began, "I'm pretty close to a semi-pro masseuse. I used to do half hour to full hour massages. I'm good with hand, neck, shoulder and just about anywhere."

"That *is* interesting, where did you get your training?" I asked with a raised eyebrow.

"Well, I'm not formally trained, but I used to finish concrete when I was first married. My hands never get tired," he stated simply.

"Woah you scored some major points here!"

We chatted as he rubbed my hands. It was nice being next to him after all the time we had spent on the phone and messaging. Eventually it got late enough that he needed to head home. He worked in Vegas but lived in a small rural community an hour to the north. So basically, he lived halfway between me and where he worked. When we walked out on the front porch, the hug we gave each other was much more natural than last time and lingered a bit longer. I made him promise to call me if he got tired on the way home. He didn't call, but I sent a text when I knew he would be close to home.

> So you give massages and do back flips and bake peach cobbler?

> Oh and you like my music and are addicted to exercise….I can think of a few other things but I don't want to overkill the moment ;)

104

I'm practically Superman. Some girl doesn't know it but whoever she is she's going to hit the jackpot.

I guess you do live in Nevada. But I have never gambled in my life...

Go ahead and overkill away.

I don't know, we've hit on something the last couple of days. I'm getting along really well with you. You make me laugh and we seem to be a good match of wits.

Bet big. Win big. Unexpectedly, I feel the same way about the other stuff too.

Momma needs a man, blow on my dice!

Hahaha. I laughed so hard I choked on my Oreo.

That's awesome! Now I want one. Of the mint persuasion.

We texted a while longer before I tapped out to get ready for bed. It didn't seem like a lot to ask, but the simple reasons I was getting along with CrossFit, 42 were not always easy to find. He was one of a long line of guys I had dated, searching for someone that felt right. There had been Temperamental Triathlete, 35 who I had thankfully only met once in person at a race. Chip, 36 whose chipped front tooth was so unfortunate I couldn't look past it as someone who'd practically been raised in a dental office. Conspiracy Theorist, 34 who was fun to hang out with but would go off the grid without warning and had some hard to believe ideas. Philosopher, 40 was similar, but mostly he just liked to talk and have someone around to listen to him. He wasn't as much fun and had pulled a bait-and-switch on me one day, getting me to watch his kids. Movie Producer, 50 was much older than his profile picture looked. Then there were the numberless, disingenuous men with shady stories about why they were divorced.

Besides, as much as I had been enjoying dating, I was starting to feel more protective of my time. School was getting oppressive again and my free time was valuable. Karate had gone by the wayside, at least for now. Michael didn't want to go anymore, and Olivia was doing dance twice a week as well as cello lessons. Jake liked to try lots of different things and had been in gymnastics recently. I had given up on piano lessons nearly a year ago. We had more going on than we could handle, but I had hopes we would get back to it eventually. To top it all off I was also going to weekly physical therapy sessions for my foot hoping I could get back to my training routine.

The next week I had a lunch date scheduled with Ms. Thomas' friend from the pool and Chiro, 44 was trying to get something on the books. The lunch with Pool Guy was nice, but I think we both realized we were lacking common ground.

CrossFit, 42 and I were keeping up via text. Apparently, the river had flooded his town blocking the freeway and canceling school. The power had gone out and he still went to CrossFit. The next morning, he sent me a selfie from the night before. He had used his car's headlights for the workout, and the selfie was of him and his youngest daughter Ivy in the glow of the lights. The text came in as I was dropping Olivia off at school, waiting in the line of minivans and SUVs. I gasped out loud when I saw him with his shirt off, the sweat on his chest and abs glistening in the light. Olivia picked up on the gasp right away and tried to pry the phone out of my hand. No way was I letting her see that.

But the best text conversation with him took place during my dental Spanish course on Saturday morning. I was supposed to be doing a triathlon, but obviously that wasn't happening right now with my foot. So, I had signed up to learn some dental terminology in Spanish. It would help with my clinic experience. It all started when he sent me a picture of chocolate covered cranberries and said:

I have found the new love of my life.

I would say my feelings are hurt, but I totally get that. Is there room for three?

Haha. I almost choked on my cranberry. Wow, is it hot in here or is it just me?

I seem to be good at making you choke on things. That's probably not a good quality for a dental hygienist, but in your case I am proud.

Oh, and yes you are the hot one.

You are too kind. You know…If I didn't have my girls you could skip your Spanish class, hang out with me and I could teach you Spanish.

> Spanish *is* pretty sexy. But my teacher is an old, overweight gringo from Texas. I think I'd do better with a different teacher. Especially if he was whispering Spanish in my ear.

> That's 2 days in a row you've made me blush. Glad you can't see this through text.

> And I'd be embarrassed if you saw my giddy reactions to your texts. So it's even.

My phone activity and giddiness had not escaped Sam, who was sitting next to me.

"When are we going to meet this guy?" she whispered.

I had already shown her pictures, but I guess that wasn't enough. In fact, quite a few of the girls were involved in my love life. I mean my divorce *had* been finalized during our first month of school, so they were kind of invested. It was sweet that they wanted me to be happy.

It worked out to see Chiro, 44 on Saturday after all. Michael was participating in the high school's Homecoming parade that evening, playing his clarinet in the middle school band. It was very hot, so Olivia and Jake didn't want to go. I didn't blame them. I let Chiro know he could join me at the parade if he would like, knowing I would be there for a long while. At least we could hang out and chat. Michael had to be there early for his call time, and Chiro was happy about the chance to come see me in person. We had a nice conversation at the parade, but it was light again. When Michael got near, I made sure to get in position for a good picture then retreated to the shade. I said my goodbyes to Chiro after some time had passed and I needed to meet Michael. Plus, I still had to go to the testing center at seven o'clock for a test that was closing that night. Later that evening, I got a call from Chiro, 44.

"I was happy I got to see you today, Melissa," he said stiffly. "I wanted to ask you about something."

"Of course!" I tried to sound cheerier than I felt. "What is it?" I had the feeling a serious subject was coming since he didn't usually call to chit-chat.

"After seeing you last weekend, I did some thinking." His seriousness was crushing. "I can't kiss you like that and then not know if you are seeing someone else the next night. I want us to be exclusive, maybe we can try it out for a few weeks and see how it goes."

"Um, you know I've been thinking too," I was not ready for this, "and I think that if we have something real going on it won't be threatened and maybe instead, we need to take a *break* for a few weeks and see how that feels." I realized I was rambling, but I couldn't stop. I was trapped and didn't know how to explain how I was feeling without hurting him. I could tell from the rigidness in his voice that I had not been successful.

"I see. Okay, I will call you in a few weeks." And he was gone.

Sensing his hurt like that hurt me too in a way, but I couldn't dwell on it for long, I hadn't done anything wrong. And just like that, I made a decision. I wasn't scheduling any more dates. I was keeping all my time open for CrossFit, 42—Drew. I didn't want him to ask me out and have my time already filled. Things were going too well with him to waste my time with any other guys right now. Drew and I had only been on two dates, and I knew it was too soon. I wasn't going to tell him my decision, not yet.

On Sunday, Olivia and I sang a duet together in church. She had such a sweet and clear voice. Before the service started, we had taken pictures outside. My intention was to have it be a family picture, but Michael wasn't interested. Jake joined in with silly faces. I loved how Liv had done her hair for the day with a beautiful crown braid. I don't know how she learned these things, definitely not from me.

Once home we had one of the kids' favorite meals, "Yellow Dinner." Jacob had been the one to name it that. It was a chicken curry made in the Crockpot and served over rice. Later in the evening they talked me into making homemade hot fudge for ice cream sundaes and they turned on a movie. I wasn't paying much attention to it, I just liked snuggling with Jake on the couch and hearing the kids' laughter.

Drew texted that evening. I had sent him a selfie challenge earlier in the day because I wanted to see him all dressed up for church. I'd sent him the picture of me and the kids from that morning. He complied and sent his after his girls were gone to their mom's. It was a mirror selfie and kind of far away so I couldn't see his face well, especially because he was partially blocking it with the phone. But I could see how nice he looked in his white shirt and tie with his shirt sleeves rolled up. Getting to know him had made him even more attractive than he already was. We texted a bit about exercise; my muscles were killing me after doing more weight training lately. Since I couldn't run or ride very well, I was working on building up my strength.

The kids left for their dad's for Sunday and Monday nights. Monday was busy with both a test and physical therapy in the morning, then pain clinic in the afternoon. I was having a hard time not being able to be as active as I would like, but my foot was starting to feel better. I thought I would quit physical therapy soon.

Pain clinic was where we were learning to administer local anesthesia. The first couple of weeks had been rough. It was scary sticking a needle in someone's face the first time, especially when it was your friend. I think it was scarier to give a shot for the first time than to receive one. Because we were each other's patients that meant that every Monday I went home numb. Once I could feel my face again, I went to the Thai restaurant for dinner and thought about the last time I had been there with Drew. We had plans to go out again this weekend, but I had to get through the rest of the week first. There was dance for Liv, a women's church activity for me, Boy Scouts for Michael, gymnastics for Jake, and I was watching a friend's kids on Friday afternoon. Saturday couldn't come soon enough.

CHAPTER 11
The Way to a Woman's Heart

It was an early morning for Drew. We were doing an 8 a.m. group WOD (workout of the day) at a local CrossFit "box" which meant he had to leave his house around 5:30 a.m. his time. As he crossed the border he gained an hour, plus it was a fifteen-minute drive from my house to the box. This time he came dressed in his workout clothes ready to go. I was in some fitted athletic shorts and a tank top. My walking boot was staying home, I had decided I could modify as needed.

"Are you excited?" Drew asked as I answered the door.

"I hope I don't hold you back with my foot, but I'm excited to see you in action!" I responded as we walked out to his car.

We chatted as we drove across town. I loved that we were both morning people. Once inside, we had to fill out paperwork and pay for our entry. There was a good crowd gathering and I was a little nervous like before a race.

We warmed up with rowing, jump ropes and squats. Drew did double-unders with the jump rope. I had never seen a double-under before and was amazed he could get the rope around twice like that and keep going for so long. He made it look easy, but I wasn't about to try in my condition. We did some lifts with Drew demonstrating for me. I had learned most of them at a weightlifting class, but

I needed more practice. I took in Drew's form as he did a squat clean. He pulled the bar off the ground and popped it up above his shoulders. Then quickly shifting his arms, he brought his elbows in and under to catch the weight as he squatted. He was strong, flexible, and agile.

After the weights, Drew helped me break down the WOD and explained what I didn't understand. I would not be doing the box jumps with my foot, but I thought I could step up and down the box fine. I would also need an elastic band to assist me with pull-ups. As they weren't part of my normal repertoire, my arms weren't equipped to do more than a couple. As the clock was counting down to the start, Drew ripped his shirt over his head and threw it against the wall by our shoes. I was surprised, but I noticed others were following suit. Several women were just in their sport bras and shorts as well.

We started with the clock, and my nervousness was forgotten as I worked hard. Drew and I had previously discussed the virtues of exercise, and one was that it was difficult to think about much of anything besides the task at hand. Working your body to its limit was a great way to clear the mind. Not exactly complaining about Drew's now shirtless figure, I stepped up and down the tall box while watching him slam out his pull-ups in succession. CrossFitters did a "kip" with their pull-ups that kept the momentum going, I would have to learn that as well.

After twenty-two minutes I was done with the WOD. Drew had finished before me and knowing he was watching had motivated me to finish strong. With the warmup and weight training included, it had been about an hour total. It seemed short compared to the triathlon training I did. They were just different. My long-distance training required that you settle somewhat into a sustainable pace and keep going in that groove. With CrossFit, pushing yourself to the max in a short time was key. Both required physical and mental strength.

We decided to grab a smoothie and I knew a place that made

great ones. Drew chose a chocolate with peanut butter and banana and mine was fruity with strawberry and pineapple. While in our workout gear we swung by a supplement store on the way home since Drew needed some protein powder. At the check-out counter, the associate had samples for us to try. Drew popped a grape-flavored recovery chew in his mouth and his reaction was almost instant.

"Oh man, this has to be the worst tasting thing I have ever tried!" He looked around frantically for somewhere to spit it.

I couldn't help bursting out in laughter as the associate handed him a small cup from another sample to spit it into.

"Yeah, I've gotten that reaction before," the associate said.

Drew recovered and slyly approached me. "You'd better try one Melissa, I wouldn't want you to delay your recovery time."

"There's *no way* I'm putting one of those in my mouth! Not after the show you just put on. Thanks anyway!" I backed up.

Walking out of the mall we kept bursting out in laughter. We headed for home and as we drove up the street to my house, Ezra was driving away from it. He'd texted that he and Olivia would be swinging by to pick up something she needed. She could get in by herself with the garage code, so I didn't need to be there. But I hadn't realized how close we would be to crossing paths until then. Ezra noticed us, but I wasn't sure if Olivia had.

At home, we took showers in our respective bathrooms and got ready for the day. Neither of us had anything else going on and were enjoying our time together. It was about lunchtime, and we decided to head out to grab a bite. As we were enjoying sandwiches, Drew motioned toward the movie theater across the parking lot.

"Do you know what other movies are out right now? Isn't there that new one with Tom Cruise?" he asked.

"Yeah, I saw the preview and it looks good. Let me check the times." I used my phone to see what matinees were playing, and there was one within a half hour.

We sauntered over to the theater after finishing our lunch. As the lights lowered and the previews began, he rested his hand naturally on my knee. Though it was a simple gesture, I was overly aware of the heat transferring from his hand to my leg. Regardless of anything happening on the screen I could not stop thinking about it. I couldn't move. If I fidgeted as usual and re-crossed my legs, he would move his hand. I didn't want him to move his hand so I would have to hold very still. After a while, I couldn't take it anymore and had to shift my weight in the seat. As I did, he moved his hand and went in for some popcorn, moving the tub near me so we could share. Ah well, popcorn was a good thing, too.

When we slowed down on the popcorn, he moved the tub back to the seat next to him. He rested his hand on my leg again and this time I covered his hand with my own. He turned his hand over and interlocked his fingers with mine. A warm surge whirled through my body. He made me feel calm and secure and at the same time my heart was racing with a sense of elation.

The movie ended, and I'd managed to follow it despite the distraction of Drew's hand in mine. It was a sci-fi film but had some romance as well. I wished it could go another hour, but as we walked out to the car Drew put his arm over my shoulder and that felt good too. Like we were together, not merely two people side-by-side.

We walked into the house and Drew stopped me in the front room which held a piano and little else. He waved me over to it.

"Are you going to play something for me?"

Pressure. "Are you sure? I'm not that great, I don't practice enough," I resisted. But I could see he wasn't going to take no for an answer.

"Well, what are your favorite things to play?" he asked.

"Oh, I like Chopin," I answered. "I play through a book of his waltzes quite often. They remind me of when I used to do ballet. But I wonder if you'll recognize this song…"

I sat on the piano bench and began to play "I Dreamed a Dream" from *Les Misérables*. It was one of the only songs I had at least partially memorized. Eventually the notes fizzled out as I forgot what came next, but Drew wanted to hear more. I picked up the piano book from the musical and finished out the song before playing another one or two.

"Okay, concert over," I declared as I stood up.

"That's one of my favorites. I love the newest movie with Hugh Jackman, it's so good."

It wasn't surprising that he liked it. Could this guy get any more perfect?

"So, when are you going to sing for me?" he continued.

"Oh, that will have to wait," I asserted. "I'm not ready yet. I would be too nervous to sing in front of you."

"Why would you be nervous? I don't make you nervous, do I?" he questioned.

"Are you kidding? When you're close to me and watching me like that of course you do!"

"Well let's work on that," he consoled as he took me by the hand and led me into the family room. "Here, sit on the floor in front of the couch. You deserve a shoulder rub after the workout this morning and you need to relax after playing for me."

He sat above and behind me and as I leaned back against the couch, I could feel his knees against my shoulders on either side. It was a little hard to relax when he put his hands on my neck—his touch excited me. I made a conscious effort to breathe out and let go of the tension in my neck and shoulders as he pressed down on them. He rubbed both sides, then focused in on one side at a time. He reached up under my hair, massaging the base of my skull and I let my head loll a bit from side to side. Then with one hand, he swept my chin-length hair back from the left side of my face, exposing my neck. He kissed me just below my ear and I could barely contain myself. I wanted to turn around but was also enjoying this moment and didn't want to rush anything. When I couldn't wait any longer, I turned and knelt up to meet his face. We shared a few gentle kisses before separating and looking at each other. I'm not sure either of us knew what to say.

"Are you getting ready for dinner?" Drew asked after some time had passed.

"That would probably be good. Popcorn isn't enough, I guess," I responded. "But before we do that, I want to tell you something Drew," I continued. "I'm not going to date anyone else right now. I'm happy with how things are going, and I want to save all my time for you. That being said, I know you haven't been divorced long and I think you should continue to date other people. I don't ever want you to question if you should have dated more and I feel confident enough that things will work out if they are supposed to. You shouldn't feel like you have to change anything for me."

He was quiet, and I could tell he was thinking carefully about how he wanted to express what he was about to say. I honestly wasn't even worried that I had scared him off, I'd felt so strongly that I needed to tell him what I was thinking. Now I would have to see his response.

"Melissa, I don't want to date anyone else," he began. "I'm happy with how things are going too, and I want to see it through."

That was it then. Third date in and we were exclusive. He came down to the floor where I was now sitting, put his hand on the side of my face and gave me one more soft kiss.

"Now let's find somewhere to eat," he declared as he stood and offered his hand, pulling me off the floor.

At the Mexican restaurant everything was the same between us, and so new at the same time. I could tell it wasn't just me. I saw the way he was looking at me and it was different. We had moved from a casual dating situation into a relationship, and I was trying not to overanalyze it. I had been honest with him; I really didn't worry about him dating others. But the fact that he didn't want to be with anyone else felt amazing. I didn't question what I was feeling and knew somehow that he was feeling the same way, too. Dating in my thirties, I had learned that who I was, was enough. There was no need to impress anyone, to pretend, or to force something that wasn't there. Either it was or it wasn't. And with Drew, it *was*.

On the drive home, we held hands. It seemed normal already, yet he had never held my hand until today. When we got to the house, he walked me to the front door but wasn't coming inside. He needed to get home. We had spent a wonderful day together and it was getting late. We came together for a hug, and I rested on him, soaking in this feeling because I knew it would be a long time before I got to see him again. When I backed up to look at him, he kissed me. As our kiss continued, I wanted more. Suddenly, Drew took me by the shoulders and extending his arms, pushed me almost forcefully away from him. Our synergy had produced a similar effect on him I surmised.

Still holding my shoulders, he said, "Goodnight, Mel," and headed to his car.

I was on cloud nine and wasn't sure I could sleep. But after the long day and all the emotions, I came down quickly and started to crash. I messaged Drew, asking him to text me when he got home safely. And then I promptly fell asleep. In fact, I slept so soundly that I didn't even hear when he texted me back.

In the morning as I got ready for church, I texted Drew:

> I'm glad you got home safely, I slept right through your text. And guess what, I'm sore already.

> That's what you get for not eating the "grape blast" recovery chew.

> Hahahahaha!

> I'm sorry about your soreness but at the same time I am happy that the WOD wasn't too easy for a tri girl.

It was a stormy morning, so I took a long hot bath. Fall was around the corner and was my favorite time of year. Since my birthday was in October that surely had something to do with it. But also, as it cooled down, I enjoyed baking more—apple crisp, bread, pumpkin everything. There weren't many leaves to watch change colors where we lived, but normally that was one of the good things of fall. Also, it was the start of the holiday season which meant candles with cinnamon and spice.

Today, I was going to Ezra's church because Olivia and Jacob were performing in the annual children's program. Liv's voice sounded above the rest, and Jake was hilarious to watch. He kept looking at me to make sure I was watching him, and he would glance at his dad as well. Michael sat with Ezra, and Amber had even come to church today. He gave me a quick wave as he darted right to his class after the program. Ezra left quickly as well, so I got some time to talk with Olivia and Jake alone. They gave me hugs and I told them what a good job they had done. After they left, a few members of the congregation came up and introduced themselves. They wanted to know if I was new to the area, just being friendly. I briefly explained my situation and what had brought me here today. When I went home, I texted Drew about the whole thing.

> The kids did a good job singing. Luckily Ezra missed all the people that came up to me afterward to introduce themselves, hahaha!

> That's funny. Hey, you owe me a Sunday Selfie, I sent you one last week. I want to know what you looked like at his church today.

It took me a minute to set up the shot. I had to prop up the camera so I could get a full-length photo of my ensemble including the slim-fitting knee length dress and high heels. After sending the picture it was a while before I heard back from him.

> Wow! You look amazing. First of all…no fair. I got your pic right as I was about to start my lesson (kind of a huge distraction). Secondly, you had to have made a scene at his church looking that good. Thirdly, he must have been regretting leaving "that." Good for you.

I was beaming, he made me feel so good! I could hardly remember a time when I had received this kind of praise from Ezra. Was I shallow? No, it really was important in a relationship to know you were attractive to your significant other. Chemistry was essential and I needed those assurances. I was happy Drew knew how to express himself to me. We talked on the phone in the afternoon before our kids made their way back to us. He had turned on the *Les Mis* movie, he said my playing had put him in the mood. Waiting two weeks to see him again was going to be rough. Olivia burst through the door and nearly attacked me for information. Who was I on a date with yesterday? She saw me in the car with someone but didn't know who it was. What was his name? Did I have a picture? How many dates had I been on with him? I didn't want to give her much info yet, but I told her that he liked the same music as me. So, she started calling Drew "Music Man."

Monday morning, I swam with No Excuses, and I decided I was well enough to try a bike ride the next day. I thought my foot could handle riding much easier than running.

Tuesday was a fun day because instead of clinic at the school, we were taking the mobile unit to an elementary school. The mobile clinic was a large motorhome with a few dental chairs inside. I took a picture out in front with my pod-mates. We had stethoscopes around our necks and looked more like nurses than dental hygienists. I sent it to Drew and he loved it, saying I could take his blood pressure anytime. I told him that I'd love to give him a squeeze!

On Wednesday as we texted about our evening plans, we spontaneously scheduled a date. Drew had mentioned that his girls would be with their mom for her birthday. And my kids would be with Ezra for Jake's birthday. We had learned about this common birthday before, but now we got creative and nailed down one hour that we could spend together with the driving time factored in. We skipped CrossFit and reservoir swims and made plans to drive and meet in the middle in for sushi. I was ecstatic that I got to see him so much sooner than I had thought.

I tried not to let the kids sense how eager I was for them to leave that night, especially Jacob. We had done a celebration breakfast instead with presents and everything, and I had a cake for him the night before so he wouldn't get sick with too much on one day. Chocolate with chocolate frosting was his favorite, and he had helped me make it. Ezra was prompt as usual, and as soon as I closed the door behind them, I locked it and headed for the garage.

It was still light as I pulled into the parking lot of the sushi restaurant, and Drew was there already. He opened my car door and we walked in together. There wasn't a big crowd since it was the middle of the week, and our table was isolated. I let Drew do the ordering. I was new to sushi in the past year but had grown to really like it. We sat across from each other, and as we talked and stared into each other's eyes, the sparks were in danger of starting a fire much bigger than the small candle on the table. Our legs were wrapped up beneath the table as well. By time we got back to my car, I didn't know how I was going to drive away from him. Before he closed my door, he leaned in and gave me a kiss. Our previous attempts on Saturday were put to shame—this one kiss had reached another level entirely. I had to take a deep breath as I buckled my seatbelt to make sure I could focus on the road.

Though it was sad to drive away from Drew, there was one consolation. We had arranged to see each other on Monday evening. Since my kids would be gone the next Sunday and Monday nights, I planned to drive down right after school on Monday. Drew was going to make me dinner. I had started to wonder about this town he lived in and told him it was about time I saw it. He didn't seem very excited about it at first.

"About that, I need to tell you something. When my divorce was finalized, it all happened quickly. We were still living in the same house, and we went to meet with the judge not expecting him to push it through that day. I had to find a place to live immediately, and in my small town it's not easy."

I could imagine that there wasn't a surplus of available real estate.

"So," he continued, "when a friend offered their trailer, I took them up on it. It's not so bad. It has three bedrooms so it's perfect for me and the girls. And it's really cheap rent. It's just a little country, so I wanted to explain before you get there. I didn't ever expect that I would be bringing a woman to my home like this."

I assured him this didn't bother me at all and that I understood his situation. But he told me he had some work to get done on the place before I came next week.

I woke at 4:40 a.m. on Friday to get in a spin class before school. I had been invited to Jacob's class for a career day of sorts, after my own classes. As I packed up things to bring to the class, I decided that the kids would also like to hear about the races I did. When I got there, we played dress up. Students wore my lab coats, masks, protective glasses, and gloves. Then I let others wear my race medals. Everyone got to participate! We talked about good oral care and wearing helmets when riding bikes. I took the cutest picture with all the kids.

Jake was full of energy having me there. It made me feel good that I had exciting things to talk about with his class and he was proud of me. I took a separate picture with just me and Jake and sent it to Drew. I found out later that he shared it with his mom as well, and she had nice things to say about me.

That evening was *The Little Mermaid* with the kids this time. We had dinner at Olive Garden on the way, one of their favorites. As we drove to the amphitheater on the other side of town the weather was so nice that we rolled the windows down and rocked out to our music. I made sure to educate the kids, so they knew good music. It was the perfect evening to be outside and the show was still fun the second time around. The producers were clever. They created the illusion that the actors were underwater by having them move back and forth subtly, gliding on roller skates that were hidden underneath their mermaid tails.

Unfortunately, by intermission there was a storm that was moving in fast with lightning all around, so we made a collective decision to leave early. If it started raining in earnest, we would be caught out in it which would be miserable. Besides we were all exhausted, so we didn't feel too bad.

When I got home, I saw that Drew had sent me a text. He told me to check my messages. We were still using our dating site message system occasionally for fun. It worked well for longer messages, more like email.

INBOX:

> I'm really looking forward to you coming to my place Monday. I will stress a little too much trying to make things just right, but in the end it's about spending time with you. As soon as I hung up the phone with you tonight, I called Summer to tell her you were coming down to see me. I think I needed moral support. Anyway, she said she wants to meet you. I'll take you on a drive around the big town

and maybe we'll stop by so she can meet you. I've got to get going, it's 11:15 and I have some cleaning to do and I need to figure out my menu for Monday.

SENT:

> Please don't stress about your place or the menu or anything. I really just want to spend time with you, and I knew coming down there was the best way to manage our time on a weeknight. It makes me happy that you are excited about it and that you have been talking about me with your friends. I would love to see the town and meet Summer. I was thinking a couple of days ago about some of my good friends I would like you to meet. ☺

Summer was one of Drew's longest and best friends in his town. She had been divorced almost the whole time they had known each other. In fact, she had helped him set up his dating profile and the dating website had tried to match them! But they were more like brother and sister. They were part of the small group that did CrossFit together most nights. Tonight, he had sent another message.

INBOX:

> I need to know what your schedule is this next month so that I can take you out for your birthday. I would like to take you to see *Wicked* in Las Vegas if you haven't seen it already. I guess I should first ask if that's something you would even like to do. Let me know and we'll see if we can find a day that can work for both of us. Hopefully I'm not getting too far ahead of myself with assuming you would like to do this. If we can't figure out a day that works,

I have other ideas too. The trick is that it is a lot of driving for you. Just a warning though, I think I still have all the songs memorized and at any point in the show could bust out the dreaded sing along.

Let me know what you think.

SENT:

3 am and that is the loudest thunder I have ever heard. So now that I'm wide awake and wishing someone in particular was here next to me, thought I'd check my messages. ☺

Wish you could've seen my response to your invitation. I popped right up in my bed with the biggest smile and gasp! I haven't ever seen *Wicked*, don't even know much about it really (except that everyone loves it). I am impressed! That you would think to take me *and* that you know all the words! That is usually my role. This bodes well for us my dear.

Time… well the only Fridays or Saturdays I have without kids in October are the first weekend or Halloween weekend. The weekend in the middle is my board review in Salt Lake City. I could also do the Mondays they are gone. Okay, not much to work with. I hope it's possible! I would totally get a sitter or have their dad take them on another night too, but we also have your kids to think about.

Drew, to me this is one of the most thoughtful and romantic gestures ever. The fact that you would even want to go has me so excited!

It's going to be even harder now to get back to sleep. But in a good way.

Saturday morning, I took the kids with me to grab donuts. The storm overnight made it feel like fall, and I got a jug of good apple cider to go with the donuts. Later in the morning we went on a short hike above our home to some Native American petroglyphs. The hike warmed us up, so we went to the gym's outdoor pool to play in the afternoon, then made homemade pizza for dinner.

Sunday was quieter at home, but we found games to play together and watched a movie. Homework and laundry were squeezed in between activities, and I got some house tidying done as well, especially once the kids left that evening.

I couldn't believe my luck—I got to see Drew again on Monday! After pain clinic I did a quick stop at home to change out of my scrubs and touch up my makeup, then I left for his house. I entered the address in my van's navigation system, but he told me to call as I came into town because it might be tricky to find his place. I got through the canyon and into Nevada as the sun was going down. Apparently, I was even more eager than I knew and my foot on the gas must have been anxious to get there as well. When I saw the police car in front of me, I figured it was too late to slow down in time, and I was right. I rolled down the window without apprehension as the officer approached. I was in too good of a mood to let this ruin it.

"Where are you headed?" he asked me.

When I told him where I was going, he did a double take.

"Why are you going there?" He looked bewildered.

"That's where my boyfriend lives, and I'm going down for dinner."

He seemed even more surprised by that but stopped questioning me. He took my license and registration and went back to his vehicle. I got a ticket, but he only wrote it for five miles per hour over the speed limit instead of the thirteen it had truly been. I thanked him and was back on my way.

As I pulled off the freeway and drove into the valley, it was quite the contradiction. Beautiful pink skies against the red desert mountains with palm trees scattered along the way softened the small, older homes mixed in with trailers. I could see a few nicer homes set back off the road in developed neighborhoods too. There was a bit of everything. I drove past a small post office, one gas station, a community center, a sandwich shop and two churches before I got to his turnoff. I had called Drew and he was making sure I didn't miss his road. At the end of a paved street, I turned onto a dirt road that curved around ending in a cul-de-sac. I saw his car parked next to the trailer, so I knew I was at the right place. The trailer was on the far side of a large grassy field. The rest of the street was filled with large, nice homes. Drew had told me that the friends he was renting from had originally intended to live in this trailer and build on the lot but hadn't gotten around to it and ended up buying a home instead.

We hung up our phones, and within seconds the trailer door opened. Drew leaned out of the doorway with a dish towel over his shoulder. He was wearing a light-colored pair of slim khakis and a pale blue button-down shirt with the cuffs rolled up. And something new—he had glasses on his face. I hadn't seen that before. I got out of the van and walked up the steps to him.

"So, you got pulled over, huh?" he asked before kissing me.

"Yeah, oh well. I guess I was too excited to see you," I replied.

Together we walked into the kitchen where he was working on dinner. The trailer was nice and cool, but dark with an older brown carpet. Still, it was clean, and he had arranged it well.

"Tell me about your glasses," I prompted.

"Oh, I forgot I was wearing these! I only need them for reading. I was using them for a recipe," he said hastily as he pulled them off.

"I like them, I've just never seen you in glasses," I reassured him with a smile.

There was a lot going on in the kitchen with an electric skillet on the countertop, a big pot on the stove, and a bowl of something by the sink. It smelled amazing.

"Thai curried butternut squash soup, Waldorf grilled cheese sandwiches and fruit salad," he announced the menu.

I looked to the skillet to decipher what was on the sandwiches. He helped me, "Gouda cheese with apple slices and grapes."

My mouth was watering with the combination of the sandwich and soup scents. He was about done and told me to sit and relax. I enjoyed watching him as he plated the sandwiches and ladled the soup into bowls. He brought everything over to the card table that served as both his kitchen and dining table.

"This all looks amazing Drew!" I complimented him sincerely.

And it tasted even better than it looked. They say that the way to a man's heart is through his stomach, but it was working for me, too. When we finished, Drew packed leftover soup and fruit salad into red-lidded Tupperware and set them aside.

"These are for you to take for lunch at school tomorrow," he told me.

"You're really trying to impress the girls, aren't you?" I laughed, knowing they would be so jealous.

"Well, it can't hurt. Oh, and there is one more thing to add." He brought over a larger Tupperware full of pumpkin chocolate chip cookies. "You can share these with the girls and your kids or keep them all for yourself. But let's have one first." They were perfectly moist with the right balance of chocolate to compliment the pumpkin.

"You just keep getting better and better," I praised him. "How did I get so lucky?"

"I keep asking myself the same thing," he said as he came over to me and took my hand to raise me up out of my chair.

He wrapped his arms around me and kissed me. *The Secret Life of Walter Mitty* was playing on the TV, not that we watched much of it. I rested on Drew's shoulder and didn't ever want to leave. Lucky didn't begin to describe how I felt with him—truly I was blessed.

"I'm getting concerned about your drive home, Mel," Drew

interrupted my thoughts. "It's dark and late and you have an early morning."

"So do you," I pointed out.

"Yes, but I'm already home. Come on, let's get your food and I'll walk you out to your van."

"Okay," I grudgingly agreed. We stood up from the couch and walked toward the kitchen.

"You have to promise to call me if you get tired," he insisted.

"I will," I promised.

We gathered the Tupperware, walked outside in the perfect evening, and I unlocked my door. Drew opened it and after I got inside and buckled up, he gave me one last kiss.

"I'll see you on Saturday," he said and closed my door.

CHAPTER 12
First Introductions

The sound of my alarm startled me from a deep sleep.

"How old are you, Melissa?" I scolded myself aloud as I groped my way through the bedsheets and stumbled into the bathroom.

I had arrived home at half past one. At least I'd been smart enough to reset the alarm for seven and had slept through my usual workout time. I was acting like a teenager but still living the life of an adult. Poor Drew had responded when I texted that I was home, and I knew he woke super early for work. So obviously he'd gotten even less sleep than me.

In the locker room after morning clinic, I bragged to Sam, "Wait till you see what I have for lunch today." I had told her the day before that I would be going down to see Drew.

"Did he send you with leftovers?" she asked.

"Yep. And it was like a gourmet meal, soooo good," I emphasized.

She gave me a knowing glance. "But how was dessert?"

"Which one?" I replied in kind, and we both laughed as we headed out to the common area where we sat to eat. I warmed up the soup in the microwave then let her smell the spiced aroma.

"Oh, that does smell good! Where did he get it from?"

"He made it himself from scratch. He roasted the squash and everything!" I pulled out a baggie of cookies, the rest were at home for the kids. "He sent something for me to share." I gave one to Sam and a couple of other girls that were sitting nearby.

Sam bit into hers. "Hey Mel, you'd better keep this one." She winked at me.

That evening after dinner the kids agreed that the cookies were delicious. Pumpkin chocolate chip was one of Jake's favorites and I sent Drew a quick photo of Jake and Liv showing their approval with cookies in hand. We got Olivia to ballet and Michael to his youth church activity. Jake rode with me, and I let him watch a movie on the van's tiny TV.

After showers and pajamas, we gathered for a family prayer, then I walked downstairs with Jacob to tuck him into bed. We usually read together from an illustrated scripture story book, taking turns. Sometimes we read another fun book, too. Tonight, I skipped the second one so I could get to my homework. I closed his door then said a quick goodnight to Michael as well. He was reading in bed, and I reminded him not to stay up too late. I went back up the stairs and Olivia and I said our goodnights.

After an hour or so at my desk, I checked in with Drew. He was home from CrossFit, and we talked on the phone for nearly an hour. But we soon called it a night since we were both tired from lack of sleep.

The next day was Olivia's parent teacher conference, so I met up with No Excuses in the morning instead of the afternoon reservoir swim. Thankfully they had planned a ride and swim which I was good for. I just wasn't running yet. I hadn't been training with them as regularly lately, so it was fun to see everyone.

After school we had a quick dinner at home. Michael had made chicken cordon bleu (from the freezer) and rice pilaf (from a box) with some mixed veggies. Still impressive. Then I dashed out the door for Liv's school though I really wasn't looking forward to this. Parent teacher conference meant awkward hanging out with Ezra as we walked around and met with the different teachers. But I got through it. The teachers did most of the talking and Ezra and I kept pretty silent between each visit. I got sympathetic smiles from friends I passed, and it was over before long.

Bedtime routine again at home and another talk with Drew. This was becoming a regular thing. In fact, we had been talking most mornings as well. As I finished my morning workout, he was commuting to work so it was convenient. Somehow the more we talked the more we had to talk about. And the more we talked about the better we got to know each other. The better we got to know each other the more we wanted to spend time together. It was easy with Drew, we seemed very compatible. But there was a lot to figure out—we each had three children and full lives. I was trying not to get ahead of myself.

Spending the day together on the weekend only confirmed all my thoughts and feelings. Doing even the most mundane activities was enjoyable with him. On Saturday, Drew wanted to find a Halloween tablecloth for his kitchen card table to liven up the place for the girls. We went from store to store till he found the right one. I needed to get some groceries, so we did that too. We ate out for lunch while running errands, then cooked dinner at my house after a short hike where we took our first selfie together. The local frozen custard shop was a favorite for both of us, so we stopped by after dinner. He had brought me an early birthday present, a piano book with the songs from *Wicked*. I was excited to learn the one song Drew had introduced me to— "For Good." The day with Drew made the wait between our dates more manageable. Still, saying goodbye was getting more difficult.

That evening, after Drew had left, I got a phone call from Chiro, 44. He was following up on our three-week break. I had kind of forgotten about that and was surprised when he called. Of course, as soon as I saw his call, I knew what it was about. This wouldn't be an easy conversation.

"Hello Melissa, how have you been doing?" he started.

"Hi! Oh, I've been pretty good, you know keeping busy with everything." I was not sure how to tell him.

STRENGTH ON THE WATER -

"I've missed you. Have you thought about how you'd like to move forward with us?" he pressed.

The direct approach was the only real option. "I have. And I need to be honest with you. I've been seeing someone else, and it has gotten more serious with him. We've decided not to date others right now."

"I see." He paused for a long time.

I couldn't stand the silence. "I'm sorry, I think you're a great guy."

"Don't Melissa. Just don't," he stopped me. "It's fine. Good luck, really."

I didn't like hearing the hurt apparent in his voice. "Thank you so much, that means a lot." I meant it.

"Goodbye, Melissa." And with that he hung up, a two-minute phone call.

During the week Drew texted me a picture of an envelope on his knee. It was from the arts center where we would be seeing *Wicked*. The tickets had arrived already! I was excited for our Halloween date; it was the next time I knew I'd see him. Hopefully we would arrange something else before that, but the next weekend we were without kids I'd be out of town for a board review course.

As it turned out, we saw each other the very next Saturday! Drew was headed up my way with his youngest Ivy. She wanted to go to the movies with her friend, so he was bringing them up for the afternoon. We arranged to meet at the cupcake place where we'd gone on our first date. I'd bring Olivia so she could meet Ivy.

I had planned to have an extra fun day with the kids. Jake got more one-on-one time with me, so I was going to take Michael and Olivia on mini dates. Jake was in my room by 6:45, my kids weren't very good at sleeping in. That was okay with me, neither was I.

"Chocolate chip pancakes?" I asked him.

He jumped on me, which I took as a yes. We wrestled around for a minute before he dragged me out to the kitchen. I mixed up batter and started pouring pancakes. Olivia and Michael weren't far behind Jake. Michael fired up his computer which was in the family room.

"Anyone else want chocolate chip?" I asked, but only Jake did.

We gathered to the table, saying a simple blessing on the food before eating.

"So, I have some plans for today," I started. "First, I have my hair cut, then I'm taking Michael for a lunch date. After that Liv and I are going shopping and for a treat. Jake, you get to do fun stuff with me all the time, so it's Michael and Livvy's turn, okay?" I wasn't asking, but I hoped he would understand. Before he could complain I said, "We can see if Crew or Sam can hang out today, or we will have fun stuff at home."

"I want to play at Crew's house," he immediately answered.

"Okay, I'll check with his mom," I confirmed. "And don't forget tonight!"

Joseph and the Amazing Technicolor Dreamcoat was part of our season tickets and started later after the sun went down. The boys weren't very excited about going.

Luckily, Janet was home and happy to have me drop off Jake to play with Crew for a few hours. So, after my hair cut, and on the way to lunch with Michael, I did just that. Michael had tried sushi for the first time recently at an Asian buffet and I had a surprise for him. I took him to a nice sushi restaurant, and we spent some time poring over the menu before choosing several rolls to try. He was quite good with chopsticks, and we had fun together.

"We should be hearing back from the school soon," I said to Michael. "How would you feel if you didn't get in?"

Michael had applied to a high school on the University campus where he would take college courses instead of high school ones for grades ten to twelve. He would also have the opportunity to graduate high school with an associate degree. The selection process had certain requirements but after that was a lottery.

"I don't know. That would really stink, I want to get in. But since the program I'm doing is newer it doesn't have as many applicants, so I have a better chance."

There were two tracks. One was general education and the other focused on computer science. He was trying for the latter which was definitely in his wheelhouse.

We finished our sushi then stopped for gas on the way home. Michael got out to pump the gas for me. He would be turning fifteen soon and would be eligible for a learning permit before long. He was growing like a weed and approaching six feet in a hurry. I called Janet and asked if she wanted me to bring the boys over to my house where they could hang out with Michael, but she said they were having fun.

Olivia and I had a few stops planned. We were going to a hair and makeup store, a jewelry boutique, and for cupcakes with Drew and the girls. Mostly we liked looking at girly stuff and trying on some things at the stores, but we didn't buy a whole lot. As we browsed, we talked about Liv's friends. Her best friend had moved away after a devastating family situation. Olivia had a new friend she spent most of her time with, but I didn't love how she treated Liv. I don't think Liv loved it either, but she didn't have the experience to know how to handle it. I talked with her about how to stand up for herself. I tried to help her understand that although it is good to help others, if your closest relationship involves you always helping them and they're never there for you, then it's not a good one.

We all arrived at the cupcake restaurant near the same time and found a booth. Drew sat on one side with Ivy and her friend Kali. Olivia and I sat across from them. We got cupcakes for everyone, but Drew and I were talking long after they were gone. The girls entertained themselves. They had started an experiment of sorts, squeezing lemons into their water cups and adding sugar packets to create their own lemonade. They seemed to get along great. Olivia and Ivy were intensely involved in their tabletop project. Kali, however, was keeping a close eye on me and Drew. She appeared a little wary about the whole situation, which made sense as she had grown up with Ivy and knew her mother well. Drew's divorce was still somewhat new, and she probably didn't understand it all.

I hatched a plan. I had five tickets for the show that night at the outdoor amphitheater. Michael and Jacob had been complaining about going tonight, so I invited Drew and the girls to join us. He got in touch with Kali's mom to get the okay, and it was all set!

Liv and I picked up Jake and went home, and I made sure to spend some time with the boys since I would be gone tonight. I got them all prepped with pizza and a movie. They were happy with the change of plans. Before heading to the amphitheater, I packed blankets because I knew it would be cold after the sun went down.

We met by the entrance and the girls took pictures together at the wooden cutouts featuring the show's characters. Drew bought them all treats for the first half, and I figured we would be getting hot chocolate at intermission. I was secretly happy about the cool night. It meant that Drew and I could hold hands under the blanket, hidden from the eyes of the girls. At one point during the show, I realized that Drew and I were staring into each other's eyes, and I had forgotten we were sitting in a crowd with hundreds of others.

Sunday was nice and relaxed after our busy day. Before I knew it, the kids were gone to their dad's. It had been a fun weekend with both the kids and Drew. Seeing the girls get along so well had given me hope for future possibilities. And Olivia was ecstatic to be an insider now after meeting Drew!

Monday morning, Jim and I went out for a ride. I didn't have any classes Mondays until pain clinic in the afternoon. We hadn't done anything together since the last triathlon besides a group swim at the reservoir, so it was fun to see each other. I had paperwork for him to bring home to Brody since he was going to be my patient next week. As we rode, Jim asked what I had been up to. I told him I had started seeing someone more seriously. He gave me the third degree, grilling me about Drew. He said he was happy for me, but I could tell he was a little disappointed as well. Our friendship had been good for both of us, and now it was going to be changing.

Driving to Drew's house that evening I remembered to watch my speed. We were both without our kids and tonight he was taking

STRENGTH ON THE WATER -

me to meet his friends at CrossFit. Summer approached me right away.

"We've heard all about you Melissa," she confided. "And you must be pretty wonderful for Drew to like you so much."

I was probably blushing, and Drew looked slightly uncomfortable as well.

"You have to know he is one of the best guys out there, so you're lucky."

Drew broke up the chat as I was nodding my head in agreement. "Well, are we going to do anything or just stand around here talking?" he joked.

The music was going already, and Drew pulled me away from Summer to orient me to the space. We warmed up and did some weight work before the WOD. The main workout included deadlifts, burpees, and sprints. The deadlift wasn't bad, but the burpee was tougher for me. A burpee involved falling to the floor and kicking your feet back behind you, then lowering yourself from push up position till your body came in contact with the floor. Then you reversed the motion, pulling your legs underneath you in a squat and jumping straight up, reaching your hands overhead. Doing even ten of those in a row was tough, but five rounds really got my heart rate up. Drew looked like he could go forever. The sprint wasn't much of a sprint for me honestly, but I hung on. By the time we finished I think I had impressed them somewhat.

As we caught our breath Summer said, "Nice job, Melissa. You did good tonight."

"Thanks," I panted. "I have a lot to learn, but I see why he likes this." Another pause to breathe. "It's motivating being together, and it wore me out."

We all chatted a bit more before turning off the music and lights and locking up. Drew made me a delicious protein and berry smoothie when we got back to his place. Then I took a quick shower and put on yoga pants and a t-shirt for the drive home. Drew pulled me into the family room.

"Come sit by me a minute," he insisted, with no protest from me. "Have you tried out the piano book?" he asked.

"Yes, but I'm far from ready for an audience. Hopefully I'll be ready to play for you in a few weeks."

My school's Homecoming week was the week after fall break, which was this coming weekend. Drew's aunt and uncle were the grand marshals for the parade and would be speaking at an alumni banquet the day before. Drew was coming up for it and had invited me to join him. I would be meeting his parents who would be there as well. His mom was especially eager to meet me, so this would be her chance. Since I was leaving for fall break, it would be the next time I got to see Drew. That made separating tonight tougher.

"I can't tell you how good it was to have you there with me tonight," Drew began. "Seeing you with my friends and how amazing you looked killing that workout, just wow. Every morning you're the first thing I think about, and you're on my mind as I go to sleep. Seeing our girls together got me ready to introduce our other kids. I'm excited for each new week, new month together and I'm already coming up with plans for you for Christmas. Melissa, I love you."

He was already holding my hands, now he released them to wrap his arms around me. We kissed for a few minutes. I was in complete agreement with everything he had said. When he backed up, I told him so.

"Drew, I can't believe how strongly I feel about you after so short a time. I feel the same way, I love you."

We kissed again, then slowly made our way outside. We couldn't keep apart. We came together like magnets, kissing and leaning against my van before I finally climbed into the driver's seat.

"Wait here, I have something for you," he said.

I closed the door but rolled down the window. He came back with a baggie containing candy corn salt-water taffy. I had brought them down in a small glass pumpkin dish for his table.

"This is to help keep you awake." He passed the baggie through the window and gave me one more goodbye kiss.

I didn't think there was any chance of getting sleepy on the drive home tonight. I was euphoric after hearing Drew say those words to me. And it felt just as good to say them back to him. I really did love him! In fact, it made me a little nervous. I was in way too far to lose him now. That would break my heart in a way it may never have been broken before. Obviously, going through the divorce had been the most painful thing I had ever experienced. But in a way, Ezra and I had been missing something the entire fifteen years of our marriage and I think that had kept my heart from completely breaking.

The next couple of days were busy with Michael's band concert and orthodontic appointment, Olivia's ballet class, Jake's gymnastics, plus my classes, clinic, and a test. But we were all excited because Thursday morning we were going to Grandma and Grandpa's. My parents lived less than an hour away from where my board review course was being held in Salt Lake City. They were going to do fun things with the kids while I sat and studied all day for two days. I was grateful for their help and glad the kids could have this time with their grandparents.

I'm not sure about everything that they ended up doing, but I did get a picture one afternoon of my three kids posed sweetly together. They had their hiking poles in hand and were surrounded by yellow leaves in the trees and on the ground. One of the nights we went to an ice hockey game with my sister Leah and her kids. The cousins had fun together, blowing on horns and cheering.

I sent Drew some selfies throughout the weekend, and we talked during lunch breaks or in the evenings. He sent me a picture of himself and Austin with a deer they had shot. I think it was Austin's first. Drew had started growing out his beard with my encouragement, and it was fun to see the progress. I really didn't hate beards and was interested to see how he looked with one.

The last day of the course, my mom brought the kids to me and had even packed us a meal. She was always thoughtful and had been a huge support to me. Almost every time something went wrong with the kids or Ezra, you could bet she would be getting an earful. And yet she was patient and never made me feel bad for calling. My parents had been very kind to Ezra, too. Even after everything. They were good people.

This review course had made the end of hygiene school feel more like a reality. I had several board exams to pass first, but they were coming up soon now. Then I would graduate and could get my license and a job. When I was in fourth grade, I had drawn a picture of what I wanted to be when I grew up. The drawing was of me as a dental hygienist. It had been a roundabout way of getting there, but I guess I was finally growing up.

CHAPTER 13
Birthday #36

It was my birthday week, so I was going to spoil myself. I scheduled Jade to come to my house and give me a massage on Monday morning. She was excited to get all the updates on Drew. Later in the week the No Excuses group got together for a birthday lunch for both me and Jenny. We rarely got together like this outside of our training, so it was fun to just sit and talk with each other. Jenny was dating someone now, and she seemed happy.

For my birthday work out, I did a CrossFit WOD called "Helen." It involved a 400-meter run, twenty-one kettle bell swings, and twelve pull-ups. Usually, Helen was done in three rounds for time. But this morning we were given twenty-two minutes to see how many rounds we could do, or what was called an AMRAP (as many rounds as possible). I had to text Drew with my results!

> Did Helen. Four rounds
> in 22 minutes.

> Awesome! How are you feeling...
> Tired? So good to get your text.

> I'm sure I will be tired, but it's my birthday so I think I can handle it!

> Haha. I feel special/loved getting early morning texts from the birthday girl.

> You are both special and loved. Oh, and missed and admired and needed.

> I hope you know how much I would spoil you if I was there.

> If it's anything like how you normally spoil me, it would be amazing! And you are spoiling me all month not just one day. I'll take that deal.

I didn't expect anything more from Drew. He was taking me to the show the next week and had already given me the piano book. So, I was surprised when flowers were delivered to my classroom. The butterflies in my stomach were fluttering as soon as I saw them come through the doorway. I knew they were for me.

The arrangement was incredible with a dozen fuchsia roses that appeared as if they were climbing their way up an imaginary trellis from the stone box. There were larger pink flowers I didn't know the name of and bold greenery to compliment. They were the most beautiful flowers I'd ever been given. Drew's brother Adam owned a flower shop in town, and they had gone all the way with this.

Not only were the other students dazzled, but my instructors as well. I felt like a princess. I made sure to let him know how amazing the flowers were and how he made me feel. He told me that he probably had just as much fun ordering the flowers for me.

That night after dinner and birthday cake I took the kids out. A drive-in movie was being shown as part of Homecoming week. They had a bunch of food trucks there for the event and we got some delicious dessert waffles to share. Jake climbed on top of the van for a better view of the movie. My kids were a little wild and I wasn't sure what Drew was going to make of them.

The evening of the alumni banquet finally arrived and I was excited to see Drew again and meet his parents. But first I had a surprise for him, and I was nervous about it. My kids had gone to dinner with their dad, or I wouldn't have attempted this tonight. When he came in the house, I directed him to the piano and had him sit next to me on the piano bench.

I placed my hands on the keyboard and let out a long breath before starting with the song's intro. My voice wavered a bit with nervousness and emotion as I sang the beginning words. Gaining some confidence as I continued, my hands grew steadier on the keys. After delivering the tagline which conveyed the idea that he had changed me "For Good" as the song was titled, I relaxed and lifted my fingers from the keyboard.

Drew gave me a tight side squeeze as I finished. Then as we stood up from the bench, he pulled me close.

"I love you," he said before kissing me. "Mel, it means a lot that you would share that with me. You are so talented and that made me feel even closer to you as I was sitting next to you, hearing you sing those words."

I couldn't respond to him beyond a nod. I had said all I could in the song, and it would take me a minute to recover.

We walked out to his car and as he drove, he asked, "Are you ready for this?"

I laughed. "Of course I am. Why are you making your parents sound so scary?"

"Wait till you meet them. My mom may be overly excited about this, so I apologize in advance."

"Oh come on, it's going to be great! Besides you're in more trouble when we get home."

My kids would be back by then and he would be meeting the boys for the first time. Drew drove us to the University, and his parents were in the parking lot as we arrived. Drew's mom was fast and got to us before we could walk over to them. She couldn't have been more than five feet tall, but she could make her legs move quickly.

"Oh Melissa, we are so excited to meet you! Is it okay if I give you a hug?" She reached up to me as I nodded my approval, and I hugged her back.

Drew's dad wasn't far behind and got in line for his hug as well. I liked them already! Drew managed brief introductions as we were hugging.

"Melissa this is my dad George and my mom Victoria—"

His mom interjected, "George and Vicki, that's much better."

His aunt and uncle that were speaking tonight were quite close with Drew as he was growing up. His aunt was Vicki's younger sister. His uncle had been the basketball coach at the college, which had recently reached university status. Now he was coaching at a bigger university in Northern Utah. They did a great job inspiring and entertaining everyone at the banquet. It was especially fun to hear them talk about their time at the college.

As we chatted throughout the banquet, George and Vicki had a lot of questions about me and my family. Before we left, I promised to visit sometime. Ezra lived close to them, so I would be passing by their house on the way to pick up the kids.

On the drive home, I wondered what condition the house would be in. Before I even opened the door, my thoughts were answered by the chaos I could hear inside.

"Are you ready for this?" I repeated Drew's question from earlier.

He smiled but I could see some wariness in his expression. The kids were running around with the boys in the lead and Olivia close behind. They must have taken something of hers. As soon as they saw us, they halted in their tracks. Liv took the chance to swipe back whatever it was Michael had and move away from them. We did a quick introduction with Jake making silly faces as I got to him. I asked what they had been up to, and the tattle fest began.

Once I got them to quit, Drew and I walked out on the patio to look at the view with what little light remained on the horizon. Olivia hovered but the boys had retreated. I should have known better. A few minutes later I heard music coming from inside. The boys had started a YouTube video of "Kiss the Girl" from *The Little Mermaid* and left it running just inside the door. They cracked themselves up, howling with laughter.

"I told you they're wild." I shook my head.

Drew didn't seem to mind but said, "My kids are really quiet. Sometimes when I come home from work, they're all in their rooms reading or something and I can't tell if anyone is there."

"Is that normal?" I raised an eyebrow and laughed.

Drew didn't stay long since he had his girls tonight. Tomorrow Vicki was going to take them to a movie so he could come to a party with me. My friends had a tradition of carving over a hundred pumpkins for Halloween, so we were joining them to carve and socialize.

It would be the end of a long day for me. With Homecoming week came activities our Dental Hygiene Club was required to participate in. We had already finished a skit competition earlier in the week along with a relay race. Tomorrow was the parade and then Sealant Saturday afterward in our clinic. Sealant Saturday was an event we did twice a year for the community. It was a way to provide free sealants for children which sealed the grooves of the molars, protecting from future cavities.

Olivia had looked forward to coming with me to the parade. The theme for the year was something to do with *The Wizard of Oz*. Thankfully I didn't have to wear anything special, just white. Drew's aunt and uncle were at the front of the parade in an open top car. We said hi to them before joining our group. Olivia and I walked with the dental hygiene crew, and it was easy to spot Drew's parents along the route. Vicki flagged me down for a picture, which she sent to Drew.

I barely had time to drop off Olivia and get back to the clinic. Sealant Saturday was always a whirlwind; three hours of rushing to get everyone seen plus the clean up after. By the time we finished, I was in a daze and wanted to get home to my kids. I had my music on as usual, but suddenly I heard a police car behind me. I looked in the rear-view mirror and the flashing of red and blue lights met my gaze. Oh great. I pulled over and the policeman followed. When the officer approached, I had no idea why I was being pulled over and too tired to even wonder.

"I've been following you with my lights on for some distance," the officer told me through my open window.

"Oh wow, I'm so sorry! I didn't even see you till now. I'm coming from a community clinic at the college and the Homecoming parade before that. I'm just trying to get home to my kids. I guess I'm pretty wiped out," I explained.

The officer continued, "Do you know why I pulled you over?"

"I really don't. Was I speeding?" I guessed.

"No. You rolled a stop back by the hospital, so right after you left the clinic basically."

I was genuinely surprised. "You *have* been following me for a while. I don't know what to say."

The officer didn't ask for my license or registration. He must have taken one look at me and found me pathetic.

"Get home. Please try to be more aware of your surroundings and come to complete stops."

"Thank you, officer. I will," I promised.

Drew arrived at six and Olivia and Jake were excited to see him again. Michael played it cool, not moving from his computer. We took the pumpkins I had purchased, as well as a dish of guacamole I'd made earlier, and drove down the couple of streets to the party. The house was full of people eating and chatting and the garage was packed with pumpkins and carvers. I introduced Drew to a few friends and neighbors before we got started on our pumpkins.

I had researched and printed out a template of a spooky house. Drew was going more traditional with a jack-o'-lantern, albeit a more complicated one. Our host had a hand mixer attachment on the end of his electric drill which was very effective in pulling out all the pumpkins guts. We carved for nearly an hour and still weren't finished. We'd have to do the rest at our homes. Drew needed to get back to his girls and I'd been away from home a lot today.

Drew came in to say goodbye to the kids and show off his pumpkin. Then we got a quick kiss outside after walking to his car door. The location was strategic as it was blocked from possible spies looking out the front window.

After the kids left for their dad's the next day, I went to my cousin Amy's for dinner with her family. We were close growing up and now living within ten minutes from each other. Her kids were similar in age to mine, though she had six to my three. She was incredibly busy but always seemed to make time for me. It was nice to have dinner with her family since my kids were gone. Amy was good at remembering what was going on in my life and eager to hear about how things were going with Drew.

"I'm so happy for you Mel!" Amy sat across from me at the table and had a talent of listening even with other things going on around us.

"Thanks, I'm having fun and it feels good with him. I'll find a way for you to meet him."

"You better!" she asserted.

Monday evening was another night of CrossFit with Drew and his friends. He had something new for me to learn. Toward the back of the gym, two ropes were hanging from the ceiling—Drew told me they were fifteen feet high. I was reminded of P.E. in elementary school, but there was no bell at the top. He taught me a technique that allowed you to use your leg strength along with your hands and arms. Drew jumped to a point on the rope just above him so that his feet were off the ground. He kicked the rope, wrapping it loosely around his right leg, then his left foot came up and held tension in the rope. He could stand easily now without using his arms much. To work his way up the rope, he leaned back and pulled his feet up the rope, almost in a stomach crunch position. Then when he stood again, he was several feet higher. It only took him three times repeating this motion and he hit the ceiling beam to show he had reached the top. The slide down was much quicker but could get you a rope burn if you weren't careful. To prevent this, he had taken a precautionary measure and wore a shin guard on his right leg.

Now it was my turn. I jumped and held on the rope above but was struggling to get my feet in the right position to assist me. I dropped back down to the floor. Jump, struggle, drop. I repeated this a few times before something finally clicked and my feet took the weight off my arms. I felt super cool. I didn't go all the way to the top because I wanted to make sure I could get back down. The descent was tricky for me too, and since my hands weren't calloused like Drew's the fibers from the rope were abrasive. I tried some more short climbs and used the newfound skill with my legs to help me on the way down as well.

After a smoothie and a shower, we turned on the TV. Lounging around with Drew was just what I needed. I was completely comfortable with him. A big part of me wished he lived closer, but I also wondered if our flame would burn out if we could see each other as much as we wanted. Maybe a slow burn was even better. I left too late and ended up pulling off at an exit halfway home to close my eyes. I slept about thirty minutes before finishing the drive. Drew must have fallen asleep because he didn't call me to see why I hadn't checked in with him. We always let each other know when we made it home safely.

I was glad that the kids were back with me the next day because our church was having a fall carnival. Michael was either a vampire or wizard every Halloween, but he didn't want to dress up tonight. That was understandable with him being close to fifteen. Olivia was an angel this year, wearing a cream-colored church dress with a golden sash that matched the glittery golden halo and golden harp she had made of pipe cleaners. Jake was Darth Vader. He had a decent collection of costumes and would sometimes wear them with his buddies. I wasn't much for dressing up but made the mistake of telling Olivia I felt like a zombie. She pounced on that and grabbed our Halloween makeup, forcing me to lay down so she could make me look the part. I went to the party in my scrubs, dressed up as myself—a worn out "zombie" of a single mom and dental hygiene student.

I had a project due at school, so the next few days I used my spare time to focus on getting that done. It was going to be a fun weekend and I wouldn't have much time for projects. I had ordered a dress for *Wicked,* and it arrived, getting me even more excited for our Halloween date.

Drew got done with work early on Fridays, so he was picking me up for our date. Even better, he was meeting me at the school first. He wanted to see where I spent my days, and I was eager to show him off. He knew Sam when I introduced her since I talked about her sometimes. I doubt if he remembered anyone else I had mentioned, but everyone knew about him. The girls would have a lot to say to me on Monday, for now they just smiled and giggled at Drew. I showed him around the clinic, classrooms, and lab. He recognized some places from pictures I had sent him. Ten minutes later we were headed to my house—we both needed to dress for the evening.

Drew carried in his suit and peeled off to the right as we walked in the house. I closed my bedroom door and laid back on the bed to pull off my tall boots. There was a long evening ahead of us and I was going to savor each moment. After taking off my jeans and sweater I redressed, starting with fishnet stockings. They weren't distasteful, these were more closely knit with a pattern of small diamonds running up my legs. The dress matched the main character of the show. It was emerald green with black buttons following the wrap of the dress from the neckline down to the left hem just above my knee. Once I was dressed, I opened my bedroom door so Drew knew I was decent. He came in before long, wearing a slim black suit and black tie. The guy knew how to dress.

"I need to touch up my hair and makeup, shouldn't be more than five minutes," I told him.

"Okay I'll play us some music," he said as he pulled out his phone.

We had been sharing our favorites with each other, but this was more romantic than the songs he usually sent me. The words "feels like home to me" kept repeating, and it resonated with me. Partway through the song I turned away from the mirror and silently handed Drew my lip liner. I leaned against the countertop to keep steady and showed him where to start. He traced my lip, and I wondered if he was too focused on his task to be feeling what I was. As he finished, I handed him the lipstick which he used to fill in the lines he had created. I pressed my lips together, rubbing in the lipstick and evening it out. He was so close, but he couldn't kiss me now.

It was about 4:00 and we had a two-hour drive to the Las Vegas strip where we had dinner reservations. Luckily time rolled back an hour as we crossed the state border.

"I have a song for you too," I told Drew. "You need to know what you're getting into."

And I played him "Dark Horse" by Katy Perry. The lyrics warned him to watch what he was falling for because once he was mine there'd be no going back. It was a little tongue in cheek, but he loved it.

In the city we got out at the Paris Las Vegas' valet parking. We were having dinner inside the mini-Eiffel Tower. As a French restaurant it started out in true European fashion with a basket of assorted breads to choose from. I had done a study abroad in Germany when I was eighteen and had spent the summer traveling nearby countries. One of my favorite things to eat while abroad had been fresh bread with cheese.

I ordered salad with roasted beets, pistachio quinoa granola, pickled kumquats, and bleu cheese. Just reading the ingredients on the menu had made my mouth water. The main course I chose was roasted chicken with artichoke and toasted pearl pasta. Drew had a delicious and tender filet mignon and made sure I got a taste. For sides we ordered potato gratin and brown butter roasted asparagus. We chose a French version of apple pie for dessert, and I was surprised when after that they brought us a platter of petit fours.

We had almost an hour before the show started, but it took some time to retrieve the car and then we had to drive uptown fifteen minutes. The art center was newer but built in the 1920's Art Deco style with palm trees in front adding color to the beige edifice. I felt like one of the rich and famous as I clicked along in my tall heels, hanging on Drew's arm. We got someone to take our picture in front of the foyer's sweeping staircase. We looked good together. The inside of the theater was impressive, and Drew had gotten us very good tickets. Strangely enough, we each ran into someone we knew and did quick intros. It was Halloween so there were many who had come in full costume. As we took a selfie in our seats, some older ladies in big hats did their best to photobomb us from the row behind.

I was captivated from the first notes of the symphonic intro. The music was incredible, and the storyline kept me guessing. I loved the spin on the classic *Wizard of Oz* and couldn't believe how good the leading ladies were. They gave me chills! At intermission we went out to the lobby for drinks and got some Junior Mints to share, then walked up the staircase to check out the view from the second floor. It was dark outside now, but you couldn't see the lights of the strip from the balcony. It seemed peaceful for Las Vegas.

The finale did not disappoint, and I tried my best to hold back tears. Drew didn't sing through the show like he had threatened but I could tell he enjoyed it, too. We made our way out to the car, moving slowly with the crowd. He opened my door for me, and I let out a happy sigh as he walked around to the driver's side. It had been a perfect evening. Drew set the mood for the drive home with quiet music. Despite how happy I was, I felt my eyelids getting heavy. Drew must have noticed because he told me to lean my seat back and close my eyes. I didn't argue and fell asleep quickly, though I was always aware of my hand in his resting on the center console.

I came to as he drove up through the winding river gorge. The moonlight reflected off the canyon walls and it was beautiful. When we got to the house, I was worried about his drive home. He said he might go stay at his parents so he could come by tomorrow as well. I liked that idea. It was very late, and we were both tired, but I wanted this moment at the doorstep to last forever. Being in his arms, my world felt right.

CHAPTER 14

On the Edge

The next morning, I met Drew at George and Vicki's home. They had made crêpes for breakfast, and I joined them. I told them they must have done something right because they had raised a cultured gentleman that took me out for an impressive birthday date. They liked that. They told me how happy he'd been lately and how happy that made them in turn. I briefly met Drew's son Austin who was living with his grandparents. It was a quick hello before he was out the door for work. He was a cute kid, and I could tell he took after his dad. Drew showed me around the house and yard, telling stories from his childhood.

Then we took a leisurely drive through the neighborhood and state park where I often rode my bike. The diversity of red, white, and black rock was stunning. For lunch we went to a burger place with milkshakes. I had learned that Drew loved a good chocolate malt. He headed for home in the early afternoon. We each had some things to catch up on and this was a good time to do it without our kids at home.

I did homework and housework and got the grocery shopping done for the week. I didn't have much to do on Sunday after church and that was just fine. I took a long nap and talked on the phone with Drew. Before long the kids were back, and my calm weekend made the transition into a new hectic week.

I had decided I was ready to run again. There was a fun half marathon coming up in December called the Baker's Dozen. The premise of the run was that each of the twelve miles you ran had to be followed up with a cookie or donut. I thought it would be an easier way to break up the run but hoped they would count partial treats because I couldn't run with a dozen donuts in my stomach. I hadn't been running in over two months, so I thought I'd start with two to three miles. Surprisingly my body felt good. I didn't always love running, but the cooler weather helped, and I liked being outside.

This week I would be interacting with Ezra more than usual. It was Michael's parent teacher conferences and Olivia had parent observation days at dance. She had two different classes—ballet and lyrical. Luckily, Ezra only came to one of them. *Un*luckily, he brought Amber with him which was awkward for both me and Liv. She never liked when Ezra and I were in the same room together and adding Amber into the mix made it even worse. Olivia danced beautifully. No one would've guessed at her feelings except for me.

I was glad when he showed up alone for the parent teacher conferences. Michael was a great student and his teachers all had good reports. One specific teacher was part of the No Excuses triathlon group and Michael said he had brought me up in class. He'd been embarrassed by that. It could be worse, at least I wasn't dating him!

I ran a few more times that week, and by the third run I was starting to notice achiness in my shins. I was just grateful that I wasn't feeling anything in the foot that had caused me so much trouble. One stolen afternoon I got in a 20-mile ride when there was a class schedule change. Masters swimming was back in full swing as well with Tuesday and Thursday morning workouts.

The girls at school had been excited to hear all about my big date over the weekend. Now that they had met Drew, they had more fuel for their fire. In clinic we wrapped our instrument cassettes in a type of paper which we then labeled with sharpies before sterilization. That week, along with my name, one of my packages of instruments had an illustration of Drew and I kissing in a grassy field with flowers all around us. The artist had made sure to identify us by name and had included a caption: "Oh love. It's a beautiful thing..."

The weekend with the kids was fun. They got together with friends and talked me into the arcade and laser tag on Saturday evening. Sunday evening as soon as they left with their dad, I left as well. Drew had invited me over to his place for Sunday dinner with his girls. This was a big deal, and I was both excited and anxious about it. Of course, I'd already met Ivy, but I was more nervous about meeting Claire. She was turning fifteen this week and I wasn't sure if she would like me.

When I arrived, Ivy said hi but was distracted by a movie in the other room. Drew was busy finishing some delicious-looking cheesesteak sandwiches for dinner. I was surprised when Claire was interested in talking with me.

"So, your dad tells me you enjoy creating art. I'm not much of an artist, but I have tried a little. What's your favorite medium?" I asked her.

Claire seemed excited to share some of her work with me and went to the other room to grab her sketchbook. While she was gone, I asked Drew if I could help him with anything and he quickly waved me off. He gestured toward Claire who was walking back into the room. I think he had noticed how well we were getting along. Claire and I talked until dinner was ready, then we continued a nice conversation with everyone at the card table. The Halloween tablecloth was gone now, and Drew had replaced it with one for Thanksgiving.

After dinner we decided to make brownies then finish the movie they had been watching while they baked. By the time the movie ended we barely had time to eat our brownies before their mom was there to pick them up for the week at her house. Drew and I got a little time alone before I had to go too. We talked about how well it had gone with the girls and planned for them to come up to my place in a couple of weekends. Drew had a big idea—he wanted to bring all his Christmas lights up and put them on my house since he wouldn't be using them on his trailer.

Monday evening, I went out for Thai instead of driving down again for CrossFit. Besides the plans we had made with our kids, this next weekend Drew and I planned to go for a hike in Zion National Park. The weather was chilly in the mornings, but I preferred that to the extreme heat of the summer. Plus, there wouldn't be as many crowds this time of year. He'd also invited me to Thanksgiving dinner with his family as my kids would be with their dad. I was going to drive up with Drew and his kids and we would stay at his sister's house. His whole family would be there.

For Veterans Day, Michael was marching in another parade with the school band. I took the kids to Chili's for dinner since we were doing a fundraiser there for our Dental Hygiene Club. The next day we went to the high school's production of *Seven Brides for Seven Brothers* which was a favorite of ours. This was one of the short weeks where the kids were home for a few days and then gone again. I used Friday to get ahead so I could enjoy Saturday with Drew.

The morning of the hike, I dressed in layers not knowing what the day would bring. It was an early morning, and my small backpack was full of both necessities and things we might need in an emergency. I had my good camera, snacks, treats, water, sunscreen, hat, bandages, ointment, and space to stash my jacket when it came off. Drew had his own backpack with most of the same things. The hike we were doing was called Angel's Landing, I suppose because it was so high up. The trail involved a lot of switchbacks but was mostly packed or paved till the end. The trees were changing colors and there were bright yellow and dark red leaves along the way. We took lots of pictures and fellow hikers were kind enough to take some of us also.

As we reached the top of the trail, there was a cliff that jutted outward giving an amazing view of the river and valley below. But to get to that view required navigating some narrow passages, holding onto a series of metal bars and chains secured in the rock.

"I don't have any interest in going out there," Drew let me know.

"Okay, well I'll see you in a bit then," I responded, not even giving it a second thought.

I didn't realize how far it was, it probably took me close to an hour to get back to him. The chains and heights didn't really bother me. What *did* were some of the frivolous "hikers" in flip flops and impractical clothing. It occurred to me that all it would take was one of them to lose their footing above me and they could bring me down with them. I stayed back, giving more room between us. At the edge the view was phenomenal! It was hard to fathom how high I was, everything below appeared so tiny. I took several pictures then made my way back to Drew. He was resting on a rock eating beef jerky.

"Want some?" he offered as I approached him.

"Sure! I know you've been stuck waiting for me, but are you okay if I take a short break?"

"Of course," he reassured me. "I'm not in any hurry, this day is about spending time with you."

As I had a snack, I showed him the pictures I had taken from the point. Then as we made our way down the mountain, I leaned over the edge slightly to take a picture of the zigzagging path and switchbacks below.

"Melissa," Drew said calmly, "what are you doing?"

I turned around in response and he snapped a picture of me.

"Quit scaring me, come away from there."

"Okay." I backed away. "You know I wouldn't have done that if I didn't feel safe," I protested.

He put his arm around me and pulled me close to him against the cliff wall on the other side of the path. "Let's stay away from ledges," he suggested. "You know, it's a good thing married people don't all know about our arrangement. I mean we get to spend every other weekend just the two of us and we don't have to worry about the kids because they're safe with the others." (This was what we had been calling our exes.) "Not that I'm an advocate for divorce, I guess I'm just happy it's working out for me to get all this time with you."

"But then there's all that time without a daily partner, that can get pretty rough," I pointed out.

"Well maybe you won't be without a partner forever," he added with a sly grin.

I reflected his same grin back at him, thinking, *Oh really?*

On the way home I posted pictures of our hike on Facebook and both our mothers were quick to respond. One of the photos was of me on the ledge overlooking the switchbacks with my head turned and smiling.

"Hiking in Zion with Drew. He made me promise to be careful, and I was for the most part," the caption read.

"I hope you are not posting this from the ravine you fell into!" my mom commented.

"It doesn't look like you were listening!" Vicki chimed in.

"You stinker! Get away from that edge!" Even Leah had joined.

The next week Jake was out of school early every day, so I had made arrangements for him to go home with friends. The schedule shortening was due to parent teacher conferences and that meant another sit down with Ezra. Fifteen minutes of awkwardness and it was done. Other than that, it was the normal controlled chaos for the week with an orthodontic appointment and oil change for the van thrown in.

Olivia and I had a special outing planned for Friday evening. The University's Dance Department had their fall concert, and her teacher was in it. In fact, she had choreographed multiple pieces and was the star of one as well. It was fun for both of us. I still felt like a dancer inside even though I hadn't done ballet since my freshman year of high school. I had never thrown away my toe shoes, couldn't do it. The boys were set up with pizza and a movie so they were happy as could be. Bringing them would have been torture for all involved.

When Drew pulled up to the house late Saturday morning, I couldn't keep Jacob from opening the front door. Jake had been so excited ever since I'd told the kids the plan for the Christmas lights. Drew was bringing up the girls and Austin was coming over too. I didn't know how helpful all the kids would be, so I made sure to have my hot cocoa maker running and ready for anyone who was cold and wanted an excuse to come inside.

I had been nervous about meeting Claire and that had gone well, but I was questioning how Claire and Michael would get along. They were two months apart in age and I hoped they would have some common ground to talk about. Sure enough, Claire got him discussing movies before too long and they were soon philosophizing about *Lord of the Rings* and the books behind the movies. Olivia and Ivy were easy. Liv showed Ivy to her bedroom, and they started making bead bracelets. Austin helped his dad the most with the lights and I tried to do what I could as well. Jake followed along—I wasn't sure if he was being my shadow or Drew's. When it was completed, the roofline was strung with large, alternating bulbs of red and white, and the trees and bushes were covered in multi-colored lights.

At some point the boys had gotten out the weapons (wooden swords their dad had made and Star Wars light sabers). Other than Austin, the kids were all interested. But before long my boys got pestering Olivia and it turned into a chase down the road. They had an audience, and they knew it. The screams from Olivia made me cringe and I tried to laugh it off.

"She's fine," I assured everyone with a smile. But I was worried they were causing too much of a scene and wondered what Drew's crew was making of it.

Drew pretended to ignore it, but there was a stiffness about him that suggested he was all too aware. We tested the lights, and they all came on with one switch inside my front door. So easy! Some of us had hot chocolate, then Drew took the girls out to visit his parents. As expected, my kids settled down immediately after they left. They could be exhausting. But I would miss them when they were with their dad for the entire week of Thanksgiving.

Time with Drew was easy. Time with Drew and his kids was easy. Time with Drew and my kids was *pretty* easy. Time with Drew and all our kids was going to be more complicated. Six kids. I was the oldest of eight and didn't know how my parents had done it. Six would be hard. But six from two different households, different sets of rules, different traditions, different parenting styles. How was that even possible?

For now, I would focus on Drew's family. I had no school starting Wednesday and I planned to get a lot done that morning before the drive up to his sister's house. I had told Drew's mom I would bring a raspberry Jell-O salad. It was a favorite of mine with raspberries in Jell-O, cream cheese, and whipped cream all layered on top of a sugary pretzel crust. Drew had told me that his family might be different from most because the men did most of the cooking for Thanksgiving. Well, I could at least make a small contribution. For years I had cooked the entire Turkey Day meal myself from scratch, so it was almost difficult for me to only do one dish.

After getting the Jell-O in the fridge, it had warmed up outside, so I decided to get in a run. I was worried about my shins and opted for a trail run, knowing the dirt would be kinder on my body than pavement. It helped, and I made it just under seven miles without too much effort.

The minivan was coming to the rescue again. We needed it to comfortably fit the five of us plus all our bags, pillows, and a cooler of food. The bonus was that they could watch a movie on the way too! It was an easy drive without having to break up any fights and without disagreements about where to stop for dinner, which would have been par for the course with my children. We stopped for burgers and were back on the road, arriving at Drew's sister's place at half past nine. Really, we were at *both* of his sisters' houses as they lived across the street from each other. Austin, Drew, Claire, and I were staying at Hannah's, and Ivy was staying with the cousins her age at his other sister Heather's. I got quick intros that night; tomorrow was going to be the bigger day.

Thanksgiving dinner was held at Adam's house. Adam was the oldest of the siblings and a great cook. Drew wasn't kidding, the men appeared to be doing all the food prep. His youngest brother Kyle was helping Adam with the turkey and George had made ten pies easily. I stuck with Drew, helping any way I could in the kitchen. I didn't know what else to do with myself. Hannah was busy creating centerpieces for the tables, and Vicki was jumping from group to group. Heather was busy with her kids, and Adam's wife was getting the tables and chairs set up with some help from hers. As all the components of the meal were completed, a buffet line of food started forming. Adam hollered for everyone to gather and quiet down, and George chose Drew to say the blessing on the food. Drew was very eloquent and said a beautiful prayer of gratitude.

Dinner turned out fantastic and everyone made a big deal about my raspberry Jell-O. But I was soon to be introduced to one of the family traditions—Hearts. I had played lots of card games, yet this was not one I was familiar with. There were three separate tables with different rounds being played simultaneously and winners moved up to a final game. I was having a hard time keeping track of all the rules. I think the most frustrating part was that multiple people were giving me directions at the same time. It's not that I needed to be the best at this game, but I was completely confused and even starting to feel emotional. I couldn't even enjoy it when I won the game. Some kind of weird beginner's luck. I was glad I'd held back the tears that were so close to the surface. Maybe I was feeling the pressure of trying to impress Drew's family and fit in.

When talk turned into Black Friday shopping, I got interested. In fact, more and more stores were now opening on Thursday evening and there were nearby outlets that would be open tonight.

"I want to go!" Ivy was interested.

Claire, not so much. "Ugh I hate shopping, but I do need some new clothes. I never have good luck finding anything."

This was my opening, both for getting to know Claire better and for getting away from the card game.

"I'm a great shopper, I bet I could find you something," I accepted the challenge even though she hadn't technically extended one to me.

Drew and Austin were game, so off we went. When we got to the outlets at midnight, I thought that maybe I had made this decision too hastily. It was freezing outside! I had my good coat and some mittens, but even so it was uncomfortable. The mall was outside so we would have to make it from one store to the other quickly. I spotted a café selling hot chocolate and pounced. It was a little *too* hot and we ended up carrying our cups around forever before we could drink it but at least it kept our hands warm.

The girls needed to shop at different stores, so we split up. I took Claire and we had great luck finding her some new sweaters, socks, and even a pair of jeans. She looked like she was having a good time and that made me happy.

When we tracked down Ivy and the boys, it was at one of the worst stores ever. This chain catered to a preteen audience and the clothes were about as obnoxious as could be imagined. Maybe more so. I came up with a contest on the spot.

"Okay Drew and Austin, I've got a little game. I want you to both go and find the absolute worst ensemble that you can and bring it back to be judged."

They did so well that the girls and I had a hard time proclaiming a winner. Austin's outfit was a black set of pajamas that featured graphics of a skeleton wrapped in pink mummy-like rags. The caption on the front of the shirt was "Total Zombie in the Morning!" and mice were weaving their way through the skeleton. Drew's was also a pajama set, but pale blue featuring a kitten holding a mug of hot chocolate and wearing a beanie with cat ears. The kitten's backdrop was a wintry forest of white and blue and there was a fur lined hoodie to be worn over top.

"I think the skeleton is worse," Ivy insisted. "It looks like it should be for Halloween."

"That's why I like it!" Claire said. "That kitten in a kitten hat is redundant and it looks like they ripped off the backdrop from *Frozen*."

"Those are both very good points," I mediated. "I think this is looking like a tie."

The girls acquiesced and we got Ivy checked out so we could head back to Hannah and Heather's for bed. Drew, Austin and I had big plans for the morning so we wanted to get at least a little sleep. My family was at the ranch for Thanksgiving, and it was only two hours away. I wanted to introduce Drew to my parents especially, and if I went up that would mean seven of the eight siblings would be there. My sister Brooke and her family were visiting from Puerto Rico, and only my youngest sister Mia who was currently a missionary in Kosovo would be missing. Austin was excited to see the ranch, it sounded like his sort of place. The roads in Wyoming were clear with no snow on the ground or I wouldn't have attempted this today. We left early in the morning while the girls were still sleeping. In fact, Austin slept most of the way with his earbuds in. And when we arrived, my family was barely waking themselves.

We made our way to my parent's condo and their door was open with one brother, Logan, sitting at the kitchen counter and the youngest, Matthew, asleep on the couch. Logan and I exchanged greetings and hugs and I introduced Drew and Austin briefly. My sister Leah came in next, heading to the fridge to grab food for her kids and a third brother Daniel came and sat wordlessly next to Logan.

"I think everyone is just getting going here. When my mom comes out then I can help start breakfast," I said to Drew in explanation.

Right on cue, my mom came out of her room and my dad came from another direction. He must have been outside already.

"Drew and Austin, this is my mom Lisa and my dad Greg."

While there was some hand shaking amongst the men, my mom approached and gave me a hug.

"Well, you must have woken up early to get here. Let's start breakfast," she said as we walked into the kitchen.

I asked how I could help, and left Drew and Austin to fend for themselves. We mixed pancake batter and orange juice, and cooked sausage in a large skillet on the stove. The final brother Gregory wandered in and sat right on top of Matthew to wake him up. Gregory was the oldest after me and was named after our dad.

"Time for breakfast, Matty."

He groaned and tried to roll over, but Gregory wasn't budging. Before things got too out of hand, my dad called everyone to order and asked me to say the blessing on the food. I expressed my thankfulness for our safe travel, this holiday, and the opportunity to spend time together. I also asked for a blessing on the food. As soon as I said amen, things went right back to how they were—this time Daniel joined Gregory on top of Matthew and started poking him.

"Alright, alright, get off me, okay? I'll get up!" Matthew exclaimed, bucking the others off.

My family was younger than Drew's and a bit rowdier. We were also closer. As in my brothers liked to basically sit on top of each other half the time, and we were big on hugs and kisses. I attributed most of this to our Italian heritage. My dad had been a missionary in Italy and spoke Italian, but most of his family had never learned the language. Other than some short phrases and mannerisms, it had been lost with my great-grandfather Giovanni. When he emigrated, Italians were mistreated, so they tried to adapt to American ways as quickly as possible. I remembered visiting my great-grandparents occasionally on Sundays as a girl and was very proud of my Italian family.

After breakfast, my dad took us on a ride in his UTV to show us the sights. I sat up front between my dad and Drew. Austin sat behind us in the flat bed, facing backward. We took trails across the property to the old schoolhouse, built in the 1800s. It had been restored and there were desks and a wood burning stove inside. My dad told us the story of when he and his Boy Scout troop had camped here overnight in the winter. The stove vent had been blocked, causing them to almost asphyxiate. They had all been safe in the end and the problem had been fixed for the future.

As it warmed up, we went to one of the upper fields where my brothers had set up a racetrack using bales of hay. They had a plan to race the four-wheelers, each taking their turn and timing it. My dad was a daredevil and my four brothers and brother-in-law followed suit. Most of them could hold their own and were close to each other's times. Austin and I took turns, and even my mom! But I hadn't known how competitive Drew was until he took his turn on the course. It was intense. He turned so tightly on the corners that one or two of the wheels were coming off the ground. A few years back he'd had a racing ATV and knew how to manage them well. When he finished, he was just behind Logan's time. I could tell he was disappointed, but he didn't mope.

We headed back to the girls after lunch. They had been having fun with their cousins and hadn't missed us. We didn't have big plans the rest of the day, but Saturday evening was going to be fun. Drew's uncle that I'd met at the alumni banquet coached basketball at a university up here, and we had courtside tickets to a game!

What I discovered that night was that those tickets came with lots of perks. For example, under our seats were cooler bags with bottles of water and soda and some candy. Drew sat next to Adam and his wife, and Claire was on the other side of me as well as Austin, Ivy, and a couple of their cousins. Just watching the team warm up was exciting! I had never been so close for a game at this level. I soon learned that Claire had an unusually strong voice. One of the opposing team players was at the foul line and the girl could boo louder than I knew was possible. She got some startled looks from the people around us.

At intermission we filed out of our seats and down a long hallway to a VIP room that was set up with a buffet of treats including popcorn, brownies, candy, soda, even ice cream! We loaded up as much as we could carry and ate part of it before heading back to our seats. The second half went as well as the first—watching these guys sink three pointers right in front of you was so cool. Having our team win finished the night off perfectly. As we were gathering our things, Ivy let out a panicked high-pitched plea for help.

"I can't find my iPod anywhere! I don't know where it went, it was right here!" She swung her head from side to side, frantically searching nowhere in particular.

We tried to calm her down and help her think it through. Then a look of realization passed over her face and she reached into her tall boot.

"Oh yeah, I remember I put it here." She shrugged and went right back to happy, sunny Ivy. The crisis was over as soon as it had begun.

Austin put together a video from the ride out to the schoolhouse and other parts of the trip. He edited it, added music, and posted it on social media. It turned out great! The drive home was easy— we had managed to avoid bad weather both ways. It had been a good opportunity to spend time with Drew, his kids, and both of our families as well. Seeing someone with their family could be revealing. I could see parts of Drew in his parents, siblings, and even his kids. I wondered what he had learned about me from my family.

CHAPTER 15
Dancing

What an amazing 4 days!
I miss you already.

I loved the time with you,
your kids, your family.

Did you get your kids back ok?

They are pretty excited to be home,
they gave me hugs picking me up off the
floor. It's good to know they missed me.

So fun to hear about your kids'
reactions. How could they not miss you?

I was glad the girls didn't seem
to be in a rush to leave my house
when you dropped me off this
afternoon. Sometimes I wonder
if they are sick of me.

> I noticed that too. I also worry about forcing our relationship on our kids. I want to spend some quality time with my girls this week and see if they will open up to me about how they're feeling about all of this.

> Good idea.

The holiday season was in full swing now. I only had two weeks of classes left followed by a week of tests and a mock board exam to prepare me for the national board in January. Interspersed with this would be a lot of Christmas parties. I was most excited for the ones Drew had invited me to. He had two work parties back-to-back on this first weekend of December. One was for his company, and the other included many other construction companies from Las Vegas. Ezra had graciously swapped a weekend with me so I could be there.

The Christmas tree went up and the kids helped with the gold and red ornaments after I draped the gold bead garland. Luckily it was a pre-lit tree which saved a lot of work. I would start to sneak in trips to my favorite stores to gather all the Christmas presents for the kids. They had given me preliminary lists, but I knew to expect some changes or additions within the next few weeks.

Jake cracked me up, he had such a good sense of humor. One morning when I dropped him off at school, we had the best little exchange.

"Have a great day buddy, I love you!" I told him as he hopped out of the car.

He turned around and looked at me seriously. "I have a deep regard for you as well."

He must have picked it up from a movie, but it was still hilarious. What a great way to start out my day.

A highlight at school was our Special Needs Luncheon. We had a class that focused on how to treat patients with disabilities and the professor always held a special luncheon toward the end of the class. It was just for the students, and the catch was that we were each assigned a "special need" for the duration of the lunch. For example, one girl would be missing an arm, and another would be paralyzed and unable to feed herself. My disability involved a tremor in my hands, but I was asked to help feed someone who was blind. My "blind" friend had her eyes covered and I would help her by putting a spoonful of food in her hand, quite shakily I might add. It was all comical but effective in helping us better understand the challenges so many people face.

I took lots of pictures during the luncheon, as I always did at school. I had been appointed the historian for our class and was collecting photos to create a virtual scrapbook for each of us. I was accruing a rather large sub folder of pictures of students who had fallen asleep in class. One day I caught our shenanigans on video as we raced clinician chairs with rolling wheels down the hallway. Then there was the carwash fundraiser, which made for some great memories. I had also started a Facebook group last year where we could communicate and share both fun and frustrations. With the year ending and only one more semester to go, we were starting to realize how much we would miss each other.

Running toward the end of the week I was in too much pain and knew I wouldn't be able to do the half marathon. I found a friend who could use my entry, and he even brought me back some swag from the event after he finished it. I was bummed not to do it myself, but knew I needed to listen to my body and give it the rest it needed to heal. The more events I did, the less I felt the need to prove anything. The events were fun and rewarding but not an end in themselves.

When Friday arrived, I drove to Summer's house instead of Drew's. She was putting me up for the night so I didn't have to go all the way home between the parties that weekend. Her guest bedroom had its own bathroom and was near the front door which made it easy to enter and exit without disturbing anyone. I got there early to dress and finish my hair and makeup. Tonight, I was wearing a red brocade empire-waisted dress with a full knee-length skirt that shot out from the waist. I accessorized with a large black statement necklace, a black clutch, and black satin high heels with bows at the ankles. I curled my hair and applied smoky eyeshadow. Drew wore a charcoal gray suit with the new tie I'd brought him. It was red with simple white snowflakes and matched my dress perfectly.

Summer wasn't around when Drew picked me up which was good, that would've made it feel like a prom date. As we entered the ballroom of this Vegas hotel, I saw they were taking pictures of couples. Prom date it was. We walked around and Drew introduced me to several people, including his boss. I wasn't nervous exactly, but it was a good thing my heels were keeping me on my toes. Most had a cocktail in their hands while Drew and I held sodas in ours. We checked out the items up for silent auction that were helping to fund scholarships for future engineers.

Before long they asked us to find our tables. We were sitting right next to Drew's boss. The table we were at was paid for by him, other tables by other companies. Drew had the steak and I had chosen the smothered chicken. As we ate, they continued raising money with individuals standing to pledge money and challenging other companies to match them. It was entertaining, especially when Drew's boss got involved. Interspersed throughout the pledges, former scholarship recipients spoke about how their lives had been impacted from the assistance they had received. When the DJ announced that the dance floor was open, Drew seemed ready to leave. We'd had our photo taken earlier and went to pick up the copies that they had printed. No dancing at this prom for us.

The valet brought the car around and held the door for me. I enjoyed the city lights as we made our way out of town. Drew and I talked about the evening and the people I'd met. I would be seeing some of them again tomorrow and wanted to remember their names and roles with the company. I was also trying to understand his job better and hoped that meeting more of his team tomorrow would help me. It was hard to say goodnight at the doorstep even knowing he was driving less than ten minutes away this time. I didn't have to wait long though. Drew was back first thing in the morning, and we made waffles and bacon with Summer. She had three kids still at home that joined us.

"How was the dinner last night?" she asked us.

"It was all pretty glamorous to me," I answered. "I had fun checking out everyone's dresses and the food was good."

"I'm sad I missed you all dressed up," Summer complained.

"Don't worry about that, wait till you see what I have." I could hear Drew protesting as I left to retrieve the picture of us from my room. I handed it to her when I got back to the kitchen.

"Look how cute you two are together! Just like a prom picture."

Drew and I laughed as we had already had that conversation. After breakfast he took me on a drive, and we had lunch later at one of the only places in town—McDonald's. I went to Summer's in the late afternoon to shower and dress again for the next party. This time I wore a fitted, navy-blue dress and styled my hair straight as well. When Drew came to pick me up, he was in a blue suit and tie. This was the third different suit I had seen him wear.

"How many suits do you have?" I asked him incredulously.

"Let's see…black, blue, charcoal, brown," he counted on his fingers. "Four," he answered simply.

"Wow. You're a really good dresser, you know that?"

"Thanks! You know the shoes are just as important," he added.

"I'm terrible about shoes," I admitted. "I hate spending the money, so I end up getting too many pairs of cheap shoes."

"Oh, we'll have to work on that." He put his arm around my waist. "I'm a great shopper, you didn't get to see over Thanksgiving with the kids. I'll have to take you sometime! By the way you look incredible." He started to pull me closer for a kiss, but we heard Summer approaching.

"Look at you two, you match perfectly!" she exclaimed.

"We may have planned that," I confessed.

The party was in a different Vegas hotel, but with about the same amount of people. This gathering was for Drew's company and had at least two hundred people in attendance. Dinner was served buffet style and was every bit as good as the night before. Different department heads took turns wrapping up the year, and the company's president spoke last focusing on the year's successes. Individuals received awards and gifts for being with the company five, ten, and even twenty years. When the dance floor opened this time, my longing gaze toward it was noticed by one of the women on Drew's team.

"Melissa, do you want to come dance with us?" she invited.

I didn't have to be asked twice. I ditched Drew and danced with a few of the gals for a while. I kept looking back at him to make sure he wasn't ready to go, but he seemed engaged in conversation and maybe somewhat entertained watching me have fun too. Eventually my feet were done, and I knew I still had to walk back through the hotel to get to the car. Everyone said their goodbyes and I even got a couple of hugs. I guess I had done okay tonight.

On the drive home Drew teased me, "You were really getting down out there tonight."

"It was fun. I hope you didn't mind me leaving you?" I turned the statement into a question.

"Of course not, I'm glad you had a good time. Besides I was enjoying the view."

"I wondered about that." I blushed, but he couldn't see in the dark.

Tonight's drive was longer. Not only was I tired from doing the same thing the night before, but I still had the drive home after we got back to Drew's. We both had commitments at church the next day. I would be helping with the children's singing time this week and had thankfully completed my preparations ahead of time. I leaned my seat back and closed my eyes, knowing Drew would keep us safe. Inside Drew's place as we hugged goodnight, I realized we had started rocking from side to side. I needed to go but was having a hard time leaving.

"Look, we're dancing. See, you can dance!"

"Nope, this isn't dancing. I can't be completely perfect, so there has to be one thing I'm not good at," he denied.

"Okay, okay, whatever you say," I gave in. "You don't have to dance."

"Phew," he exhaled, then kissed me.

I needed to get going, I had another hour before I'd be home. This time I made it within fifteen minutes from home and had to pull over. I exited the freeway then turned into a small neighborhood by the high school. I couldn't keep my eyes open any longer. I was probably only there for twenty minutes at the most before I woke up and drove home. As I started driving, I received a text from Drew who was wondering if I had made it home yet, thinking I had forgotten to let him know. When I got home, I called to explain why it took me longer to text him. He was glad that I had stopped. Both of us must have been quite smitten to do all this driving.

This week at school would wrap up the semester and I had some tests and a presentation to complete. I was lucky that my kids were used to a routine so that once they got to bed, I had a couple of hours of uninterrupted study time. I took it one day at a time, preparing for what was coming up the soonest. By Thursday I was done with my school commitments, but I had one more test to take—a mock board for the first of three board exams.

This first exam was the written board which I would be taking in a few weeks in Las Vegas. The review over fall break had helped me prepare well. The second and third boards would be clinical, and I would travel to another state to test. The second was for local anesthesia and would be evaluated by me injecting one of my fellow students in multiple sites while being watched. Then I would take my turn being injected for one of them. The third board was the general clinical board which was scheduled at the same site on the next day. We were required to clean a certain number of teeth, and those teeth had to qualify by having enough difficult plaque and tartar for us to remove.

Finding the right patient could possibly be the hardest part of the whole process. Too easy and they wouldn't qualify, too hard and you could fail. My plan was to create business cards and drop them off at the local free clinic soon to find someone that could use a free cleaning. The type of cleanings needed for these qualifying patients could be expensive without dental insurance at a regular office. We had grants at the school that helped, and patients that agreed to travel for the boards were compensated by us for their hotel, travel, food, and sometimes more beyond that.

There was a fourth board which I was not taking. Only three out of the twenty in our class had chosen to sign up for it. This exam was for expanded functions which meant placing silver and tooth-colored fillings. This was only allowed in two or three states, and not anywhere I planned on living. The board was in the northwest, and I didn't want to spend the money on it. Honestly, I just didn't want to do expanded functions in general. This had been one of my least favorite and most stressful parts of school and it was okay with me that I wasn't going to be licensed for that.

> Off to my mtg but thinking mostly about you.

> Trying to study but thinking mostly about you.

> Maybe I should give you a test about me. Then you could do both at the same time.

> I would need to spend lots of time with you to prepare.

I finally buckled down and took the mock board online. As students we were all aware of what was required to pass each exam, and for this one I needed 75%. The test was split into two portions, and I got 70% and 68%. That made the combined score 69%, but the good news was that this was considered a "raw score" and fourteen to sixteen points would be added to that to become the "standard score". Each year, several questions were thrown out including a certain percentage of questions that were experimental. So, I'd passed the practice test with at least an 83%.

The Christmas parties for this week were for school and the triathlon club. There was an old roller-skating rink with a wood floor, and this is where our classmates had decided to get together. Our instructors and significant others were invited as well. Drew came up, and it was fun to show him off again. I did my historian duty and made sure we got pictures all together. The next party was later in the week for the local triathlon club and was a dinner in one of the rec center's extra rooms. It was fun to hang out with everyone and I walked away with some cool prizes, too!

Saturday there was a pancake breakfast at church and Drew came back for that. My kids weren't with me, but it was fun that some of the families were dressed in Christmas pajamas. I introduced him to lots of people and he impressed everyone by helping clean up at the end. We planned to do some Christmas shopping during the day and Olivia had a dance recital in the evening. I got to learn what a great shopper Drew was after all. He was nervous if I ever set my purse or shopping bags down, so he carried them for me. Before long he was weighed down, but it didn't seem to hold him back. Then I spotted something that made me laugh so hard.

"Look Drew, it's you! You'd better let me carry a couple of those bags."

There was a male mannequin wearing a long sleeve shirt that disguised the origin of the problem, but it's left arm was much longer than the right.

"I wouldn't want you to turn out like that guy."

For some reason I thought this was hilarious and made Drew stand next to the mannequin for a picture. It was good to get this shopping done though. It was less than two weeks to Christmas, and I would be taking the kids up to visit my parents the weekend before.

That night at the dance recital Drew got his first real look at Ezra and Amber. We didn't exactly do introductions, but they were there with my boys and her kids as well. As soon as the last number was finished, I hustled down the hallway to where the dancers would come out from backstage. I wanted to give Liv a hug before her dad got there so I could get away clean. No such luck. I saw Ezra approach and do one of those head jerk acknowledgement moves men do to each other.

"Hi, you must be Drew." Ezra extended his hand as he introduced himself.

"Good to meet you, Ezra."

Drew was so at ease with this situation I was surprised. These guys could have been buddies from any onlooker's perspective.

"Olivia danced very well tonight, you must be proud."

"She's really something, isn't she?" Ezra agreed.

"Olivia is such a natural dancer, she's so fun to watch!" Amber jumped in.

What was going on here?

"She is," I went along with it. "She really lights up the stage."

I was squirming inside, and I could tell Olivia was too though her stage smile was convincing everyone.

"Good job Livvy, you did so well." I gave her a squeeze and backed away.

I was ready to get out of here. I said lightning quick hellos to the boys and then it was goodbyes. It took all my self-control to not run as I turned around. I wanted to get away from this situation. It was all fake and I hated it.

I knew Drew could feel my anxiety as we walked away. He grabbed my hand and squeezed it tight, but we didn't talk until we got outside the doors of the high school.

"Are you okay?" he asked me.

"Yeah, I just don't like that stuff. How were you so relaxed?" I marveled at his cool demeanor.

"Why wouldn't I be?" He exuded confidence.

"I don't know, but if it was your ex, I think I would be a basket case."

Drew let out a good-natured laugh. "You have nothing to worry about there either. She and I have been done for years, well before the divorce. No feelings left. And you and Ezra are done too, right?"

"Of course! But I still feel weird around him. And with Amber there it gets worse, I guess. So much going on. And the kids. And—"

"It's okay Mel."

We were at the car, and he opened my door but stopped me to look me in the eyes.

"It didn't bother me at all and you're stronger than you think. I don't care about any of them. Just you." He made all the anxiety melt away.

"You're right, it doesn't matter." I could be confident like him. "I love you, Drew."

"I love *you*, Mel." He gave me a kiss and helped me into his car. He made my heart dance.

CHAPTER 16
Christmas Crisis

I had one week to myself before the kids were out of school. I did more shopping, went to lunch with Janet, and got my life organized at home. I also raked the leaves in the yard. A fall chore in the winter—living in the desert could be strange. It was nice to be home more, and it meant that Jake didn't have to go anywhere before or after school. We were all going to get some quality time over the next couple of weeks.

I brought lunch to Michael one day at school and took Jake swimming. Olivia did some shopping with me. By time the weekend arrived I had all of Christmas wrapped and either under the tree or waiting for stockings. The big present was hiding in the closet behind my dresses. It was a new TV since ours had a big line through the picture and was almost impossible to watch anymore. I even had gift bags for Drew and his kids next to my bed.

When we visited my parents, my California Grandma was staying with them, so I got to spend time with her. And my Granny came over for dinner one night, too. I saw most of my siblings except for my two sisters who lived away. Leah and I took our kids to the aquarium, and Logan's wife Lauryn came too. She loved animals and knew a lot of fun facts about them. We visited the Christmas Village downtown that was covered in lights and featured tiny houses with

Christmas scenes. It was very cold that night, so we didn't stay long. My blood wasn't used to these temperatures anymore. We watched Christmas movies, and my parents gave their presents to my kids. My mom had nice things to say about Drew, but she also had a lot of questions. I think she was holding back a bit, trying not to get too attached yet. I texted Drew about it.

So, what questions did your mom have for you?

She was wondering if we have had any more serious conversations.

Haha. Your mom is awesome. But now I'm curious...what was your answer?

I said no we haven't. What else would I say? She did ask if I thought you would surprise me sometime and propose. I said I didn't think so, that we have a few more important conversations to have first. Maybe we should wait a couple of years. ;)

Hahaha!! Do you think I could really last that long? Remember I was teasing you about drive thru wedding chapels after about six dates.

I'm just wondering how I can survive the next day till I get to see you!

We got back home the day before Christmas Eve. So, Christmas Eve Eve. I ran to the grocery store to get a few last things for Christmas Eve dinner and breakfast on Christmas morning. The plan was for Drew to join us for dinner, then he would stay at his parent's house and be back on Christmas morning. His kids would be with their mom until one o'clock on Christmas Day, then he would pick them up. My arrangement was different than his. I had my kids for the entire first half of their winter break, then they would go with their dad. So, this year they were with me for Christmas and with their dad for New Year's.

Drew arrived in the afternoon on Christmas Eve. We watched a Christmas movie together with the kids as I finished preparing dinner. It was a traditional ham with cheesy potatoes, corn, fruit salad and homemade rolls. The boys wolfed theirs down as they usually did and jumped up from the table to run away. I stopped them and had them clear their dishes. I could tell Drew was surprised by their early exit. I'd noticed his girls ask to be excused from the table when they finished eating. Olivia stayed with Drew and me until we finished, she was a slower eater. Plus, I knew she wanted to spend more time with us. Drew helped with the dishes, and I put away the leftovers.

"Mom, mom, can I open a present?" Jake pestered.

"I'm still cleaning bud, you're going to have to wait. Remember you only get one tonight."

"But can I open it now?" he persisted.

"No," I said more firmly. "You will have to wait. I think we're going to go for a drive first anyway to look at Christmas lights."

He walked away slowly.

"Yikes," I said to Drew. "He has a one-track mind."

We finished in the kitchen, and I hollered at the kids to get in the van. We had 3D glasses that were specific for looking at Christmas lights. They projected images onto the lights such as candy canes or reindeer. There were some neighborhoods that always had impressive lights and I headed that direction. Drew was in the front by me.

Two minutes into the drive Jake was out of his seatbelt, and I told him to get back in it. Then a few minutes later he was whining that he wanted a specific pair of glasses that Michael or Olivia had. It was something else only moments after that. I didn't know what was going on, but he was in a mood. It put all the rest of us on edge. The other kids were annoyed with him, and I couldn't do anything from the driver's seat. Eventually I switched Drew so he could drive, and I climbed in the back. This wasn't turning out to be the family bonding activity I had envisioned. When we walked in the door from the garage, Jake immediately picked up on the thread he'd started after dinner.

"Now can I open a present Mom? You said after lights, so now can I?" He was relentless.

"You just get one. What are you so eager to open?" I asked him curiously.

He picked up a small square present with his name on it. I knew it was a video game that he had asked for a long time ago, something with racing trucks. I really didn't think he remembered asking for it and wondered what he thought it was.

"Okay if that's the one you want to open, we will do the rest tomorrow."

He ripped off the paper and instantly broke into tears. "This isn't what I wanted! I didn't even ask for this." He threw the game across the carpeted family room and went back to the tree. "I want to open another one."

"You're not supposed to know what everything is, that's why we wrap them. And you did ask for that game a while ago," I tried to reason with him.

"No, I didn't!" he refused. "I don't want it! I wanted another game."

"Well, maybe you'll get another one tomorrow but acting like this isn't going to get you another present tonight. That's not how it works. Look, we have new pajamas, too. Let's get those on." I walked him to his room.

I didn't want to do this anymore in front of Drew. I was embarrassed I couldn't control my own children and was worried what he was thinking right now. I left Jake to get on his pajamas and walked back out to watch Michael and Olivia open their one present each. They were happy with what they opened, and Jake walked out just as they had finished. I gave Michael and Liv their pajamas to get on and told everyone to say goodbye to Drew, then I walked him outside. I let out a big sigh after I closed the front door.

"I'm sorry it has been so out-of-control tonight. Jake was on one," I apologized.

"It's okay," Drew said, though he looked like a deer caught in the headlights. "I bet tomorrow morning will be better." He was optimistic.

I gave him a hug and kiss and he left. Walking back through my front door felt like a weight pressing down on my shoulders. Sometimes I wished I could escape all responsibility and live a fairy-tale life with Drew. Of course, that wasn't practical or even what I really wanted, but the everyday navigation of parenting was exhausting. And on nights like tonight, it seemed like I was failing. I gathered the kids, and we said a family prayer under the glowing lights of the Christmas tree. I was hoping, like Drew had said, that tomorrow would be better.

After tucking the kids in bed, I assembled the breakfast roll ring in a Bundt pan and covered it with a dish towel so it could rise overnight. Pulling out the hidden presents, I arranged them around the stockings. They had each chosen a place on one of the couches to set their stockings, and I filled them in my bedroom before putting them back where they had been. The TV went between the tree and the wall, I wasn't about to attempt wrapping it. I climbed in bed and was asleep before I even had time to think. Too tired to obsess over anything right now.

I woke to a happy Jacob bounding through my bedroom door. He climbed up on the bed and started tugging on me to come out with him.

"Santa came Mom, I already looked in my stocking. There's candy and stuff in there! And presents, too! More presents! Can we open them?" Jake's enthusiasm could not be contained.

"Really? Yes, we can open them, but let's go get Livvy and Michael first, okay?" I stalled, checking on my hair and face quickly, knowing Drew would be by sometime soon.

Jake ran out, presumably to go wake his siblings. We all made our way into the family room at about the same time. Jake didn't ask permission again. Now that we were all here, he started ripping off paper from his presents.

"Look Mom, look! I got the Lego Batman game!" He waved it in my face. "And the Lego Batman was in my stocking. Look, look!" He put them together to demonstrate that they were a pair.

"So cool, buddy. Was that what you were hoping for last night?" I wondered aloud.

"Yes, but I didn't know Santa was bringing it!" He was ecstatic.

Michael and Olivia were more subdued as they opened other games, movies, art supplies, clothes, etc. Michael had noticed the TV right away but kept quiet. When Jake got to the big box, he revved up again.

"Mom! Santa brought us a new TV cause our old one is broken! He knew it!" He tugged on my sleeve.

"You're right, that's exactly what we needed! I'm glad we won't have to look at that line in the TV screen anymore. And it'll be better for your games, too, right?" I played along.

Jake agreed, and soon he had recruited Michael to help him open the box. While the boys were tracking down scissors to use on the box, and I was putting breakfast in the oven, there was a knock on the door. I unlocked and opened it for Drew. He looked much better than I did, all dressed and ready for the day.

"Jake's in a much better mood today," I quietly updated him.

"My prayers must have worked." He smiled back at me.

"Drew, Drew, Santa brought us a new TV! Will you help us open it?" Jake pulled on his arm.

"You bet. Do you have a knife or scissors?" He walked across the room.

I took the opportunity to check in with Olivia. I had her show me what she had unwrapped, then she asked about my presents.

"Oh, I haven't even looked," I told her. I knew there were a few things I had wrapped up with my name and I had filled my own stocking.

"Here's one!" She handed me one of my presents.

I knew it was a pair of fuzzy socks—I wore them constantly through the winter. I opened it up.

"Santa knows me well," I remarked. "And my old socks *are* getting worn out." Before I had the chance to open another of my presents to myself, Jake came running up to me.

"Mom, Drew brought some presents, too. Can we open them?"

I looked to the pile he had brought in with him. "Sure, but let's wait till Drew can watch. He's busy with the TV." He and Michael were at that moment pulling it out of the box, but he had heard the conversation.

"Let's open my presents then we can set up the new TV," Drew said as he brought over his gifts. He handed one to each of the kids, then one to me as well.

He'd done a good job. There was a small Lego set for Michael, some putty and nail polish for Olivia, and a movie for Jake.

"Now it's your turn, Melissa," he prodded.

"Hmmm, wonder what this is?" I slowly removed the wrapping paper revealing a shoe box. "Shoes? But what kind of shoes?" I looked inside and they were CrossFit specific shoes, very nice ones. I was impressed. "Wow, thank you! These are so nice and now I can look the part when I do CrossFit! Plus, they will make me way better, right?"

Drew laughed and made me try them on to make sure they fit, which they did.

"Now it's your turn." I gestured to the last present under the tree. He went and picked it up and the kids watched as he unwrapped. It was nothing special, a hat from his favorite NFL team and a button-down shirt.

"Thanks Mel, I love them," Drew said.

Gifts weren't really my thing. I liked getting things for others, especially when I could find the perfect gift. It was just so much pressure and I'd rather buy myself the things I wanted. I always made the kids give me specific lists, so I knew I was getting what they hoped for. But Drew had done well picking my present. I probably wouldn't have spent the money on myself for those nice shoes.

Drew and Michael moved the old TV then put up the new one, connecting it and running through the installation process. Once it was connected to the satellite and he could see it was working he turned to me.

"I'd better get going." He stood and collected his things.

"Yes, you need to get there before your kids. I'll bring down my presents for them." I walked him to the door as the kids yelled goodbye. "Tomorrow?" I asked.

"Yeah, I'll call so we can work out the details."

Drew and I had plans to meet the next day at the movie theater with all our kids except for Austin. Unfortunately, we couldn't get them all to agree on one, so we ended up splitting our group and went to two different movies at the same time. Drew and I went with Jake and Michael, and the girls went to the second movie. We supplied everyone with popcorn, candy and drinks then headed into our respective theaters. Our movie ended first, so we found a bench to sit on while we waited. Jake came and forced his way between me and Drew. I wasn't sure if it was because he wanted to be by both of us or because he wanted to separate us.

The next day was a big day for Drew and his family. Austin was finding out where he would be assigned for his two-year missionary service. There was a big gathering of family and friends as he opened the envelope containing the assignment, and they assembled in Drew's ex-wife's home. I wasn't disappointed not to be there. It would have been awkward and honestly, I don't think it would have been appropriate. But it was exciting to get his text with the news.

> Atlanta, Georgia!! He leaves
> February 11.

> Awesome! He was guessing East,
> but more Southern than he predicted!

I drove down to Drew's on Monday afternoon. I was staying with him and his girls for the next few days since my kids were gone for two weeks. Drew set me up in his room and he would sleep on the couch. The first day we went grocery shopping and watched a movie after dinner. The next morning, Drew and I went to CrossFit, then in the afternoon he and the girls introduced me to Valley of Fire State Park with its red rocks that looked aflame. The car trip with the girls couldn't have been more different than the one on Christmas Eve with my kids. They were mostly quiet but piped in when we directed the conversation to them.

"So, what is one of the best parts of the park to see?" I asked them.

"Elephant Rock!" Ivy exclaimed.

Claire agreed but added, "I also like the petroglyphs. And there's another good hike but it's longer and maybe it's too cold today."

She was right, I didn't feel like doing a long hike today in the chilly temperatures. I handed the girls a baggie of saltwater taffy that was in my purse. They each chose a few and passed it back. Elephant Rock was barely inside the boundaries of Valley of Fire, not far from Lake Mead which I had visited many times with my family growing up. Drew parked and we got out, zipping up our jackets against the wind. Claire led the way with Ivy just behind while Drew and I straggled a bit. There were several caves and openings in the rocks, and we ducked inside one to get out of the wind.

"Let's take a picture," Drew said as he pulled out his phone.

Pressing the button to switch to selfie mode, he held up the phone and snapped a quick picture. Later when he texted me the picture, I noticed that Ivy had her mouth full of taffy. She looked like an adorable chipmunk. We braced ourselves and walked back out into the wind.

Claire pointed and said, "See the elephant?"

I *could* see it. There was a tall, long rock that was separated from the body of the elephant, forming its trunk. Claire and Ivy ran all the way up to the elephant. I took some pictures from a distance so I could take in the whole thing. They ran back to us before long; it was much too cold for gallivanting. We drove through the main road of the park taking in the sites before returning home.

"Hot chocolate?" I asked as we got close.

"Yes!" the girls sounded in unison.

We made hot chocolate with mini marshmallows on top and started the next of *The Lord of the Rings* series. Claire knew everything about the movie and the characters. I had read the books, so I had some interest, but was not at her expert level.

The following day was New Year's Eve and the girls had plans. Claire would be back after midnight and Ivy would be sleeping over. Drew and I ended up at the home of his friends just talking and eating, we had made brownies to contribute. We picked up Claire on the way home and snuck in a New Year's kiss after she went to her room.

New Year's Day, I headed home. I didn't want to monopolize all of Drew's time with his girls and I had a wedding reception for a classmate the next day. But after the longer visits with Drew, I missed him more.

> You really are wonderful Drew. I love you so much. I enjoyed making more memories with you this week.

> I hope that I can be the guy that you have always dreamed about and wanted.

> You are better than I have ever dared dream for. And want? I want you more than anything.

> I think we have a lot of good things in store for us.

The wedding reception was fun, and I managed to sneak in some time with my kids the next week. Ezra was working, so he was okay with me taking them to lunch. I took them individually on separate days so we could get one-on-one time. I worked out, got the van in to fix a recall I had received a notification for, and did some last-minute studying. Then I left for Las Vegas. The testing center for the written national board exam was there and I planned to have a mini vacation. I booked time at the day spa and got tickets for a Cirque du Soleil show.

The testing center was intense with very tight security. It made me feel nervous even though I was obviously not doing anything wrong. The test was scheduled for three hours in the morning and three in the afternoon with time in between to grab lunch and recharge. With the first questions I agonized over every little thing, and by the end I was almost ready to pick at random. The brain could only handle so much.

Drew's girls were with their mom this week, so he was free to come take me to dinner, which he did. I had an hour or so to recoup in my hotel suite before he showed up. We went to an Italian place nearby and I started to relax. It was settling in that I could now enjoy the next couple of days. There was nothing more I could do to change the test score at this point, and it would be weeks before I heard back.

The following day I went to the spa in the hotel and spent a good five hours there. I rotated from hot tub to reclining chair to the lounge to munch on healthy snacks. Nothing but a bikini, a big robe, and my book. This was my kind of day. The spa was divided by gender, so there were women that didn't even wear a bathing suit. That was out of my comfort zone. I averted my eyes and stuck to my book when they got in the hot tub. As it got later, I showered with all the fancy soaps, razors, and lotions available and sat at one of the nice vanities to do my hair and makeup. Then I collected my belongings from the locker area and went up to my room to wait for Drew.

He arrived less than an hour later, and we went out for Thai this time before going to the Cirque show. The show was based on the music of the Beatles and the small round theater made it easy to see everything. But there was so much going on at any given time, you could never really watch it all. My cousin (Amy's brother) was part of a Cirque show in Orlando and I wished he was in this show instead so I could watch him. He had always been a talented tumbler when we were kids.

When the show ended, we went back to my suite. We were grown adults with no one to give us a curfew or tell us what to do. It was only our belief in the sanctity of marriage that kept us from doing what our bodies so naturally wanted. Luckily, Drew had work in the morning, so at least we had some time restraints. It wasn't an easy thing to stop the progression of passion when our hearts and souls felt completely connected. I really loved Drew and I knew he loved me too.

In the morning I treated myself to the breakfast buffet at the hotel, trying some of everything that looked good without going overboard. Then I packed up and checked out, driving the two hours to home. Drew was at work in Las Vegas today and driving away from him felt wrong. Everything in me wanted to go toward him.

CHAPTER 17
It's Complicated

It was Michael's fifteenth birthday and he wanted to host a LAN (local area network) party that weekend. From what he explained to me, he hosted a server and his friends each had their own computers but connected them to the same local network for playing games. What any one of these kids could do was completely over my head. We had received the good news that Michael had been accepted into the program at the University where he would be focusing a lot on computer courses. A couple of his friends had been accepted as well; I was happy for him.

On the other hand, Michael attending this school could be a complication. The closer Drew and I got, the more I was thinking about the future. I had been poring over my divorce decree and the legal ramifications of a move should we get married. According to everything I could find, I should be able to take Olivia and Jacob with me for this short-range move. It was under the allotted miles in the decree. I knew it would change our schedule, but I was the primary household for the kids and thought that would be allowed to continue. Ezra would still have them every other weekend and maybe more in the summer or on holidays if it was too far for them to stay with him during a school week. But even though I would miss the daily time with him, I wouldn't want Michael to give up his opportunity and knew he would be happy living with his dad.

Drew and I had been discussing this more too. We had gotten to the point that we needed to know if *we* were possible or not. I didn't want to get my heart broken, so I couldn't keep moving forward if we weren't going to be able to make it work with our kids. It wasn't practical for Drew to move. His job was in Las Vegas and commuting more than an hour was out of the question. The only real option would be for me to move to him which would require moving my kids from their schools. I thought Olivia and Jake would do okay in this scenario, they were young and could make friends easily. They needed to be with their mom more than their friends, and I knew Drew would be good for all of us. Having a stable home where they could have a father and mother figure and watch a healthy relationship would help them as they had their own relationships in the future. From the bits and pieces I was picking up from the kids, I wasn't sure they were getting this in their dad's home. Then one day at church, the mother of Olivia's friend Erin came up to me as the women's class finished.

"So, I heard about Ezra and his wife. How are you doing?" She had a concerned expression on her face.

"Heard what?" I was confused and from the change in her face she saw that.

"Um, Olivia told Erin that they're getting divorced." Her eyes widened as she realized I didn't know. She scrambled, "I thought you knew, I didn't know that Olivia hadn't told you. She must have been worried about how to tell you. Oh, I'm so sorry, I didn't mean to overstep." She didn't know what to do because now I was crying.

He was getting divorced? Why hadn't anyone told me? I knew it hadn't been sounding good, but divorced already? It hadn't even been a year—what was going on? It was like I was getting the news about my own divorce all over again. I was devastated and it didn't even make sense. I mean, this wasn't my marriage falling apart, it was Ezra and Amber's. Why did it matter so much to me? I couldn't process it. It seemed like a waste, all for nothing. Why did our kids have to go through this again? Was there nothing that would work out for our family? I tried to pull myself together, the kids would come looking for me soon.

I ached for the kids and their emotional rollercoasters and was selfishly upset thinking that Ezra and I should have just stayed together and worked things out. Had we really been beyond all hope? My feelings and thoughts were jumbling together and not making sense. I was somehow aware of that, but I had no control of them. I held it together until the kids left for their dad's that evening and then I lost it completely. It was getting to the point that I didn't even know what I was crying about anymore.

Drew texted me to see if the kids had left so we could talk, and I managed to text him back that I had a headache and was going to take something and go to bed. It wasn't a lie exactly; I had developed a headache at this point and needed to sleep to make it stop.

But in the morning, it wasn't gone and was compounded with voices in my head. Ideas were circulating that were dark and angry and hopeless. I didn't know how to make them go away. Usually, I called Drew after my workout, but I had slept in and missed him. That was for the best, and he was sure to think I was sleeping off my headache. I had to rally and get to school. There was no time to wallow in whatever this was. When I got to school, Sam could see right away that something was wrong.

"You okay, Melissa?" she asked me.

"Yeah, I got a bad headache last night and didn't sleep well," I told her, omitting the real reason for why I wasn't feeling well.

I could barely focus on my lectures that week. It was all business with my patients, and I was going through the motions at home. I didn't take it out on anyone, it's just that I was having a hard time feeling any joy in my life right now. Drew and I talked as usual, but I think he could probably tell that something was wrong. The reasons for me to be unhappy were piling on. I had orthodontic and vision appointments for the kids, the van had to go back in for work, I was wasting money on renting Michael's clarinet so bit the bullet to buy one, and on and on. I felt like I was being buried alive.

When the kids left on Friday, I collapsed and curled up on the floor. I thought my heart would burst. I knew I should call someone to talk but also knew I couldn't possibly get words out right now. All I could get out was *help me, help me.* I was calling to God. I knew he could help, I just didn't know how.

Feelings of inadequacy and doubt washed over me till I thought I would drown in them. I had stayed true to my commitment to God—I was saving myself for marriage, but I hadn't been a perfect angel either. Why would he want to bless me with Drew? This was all bound to fall apart and I should wall up my heart now to protect myself. Ezra's marriage was failing, what made me think *I* could pull it off?

No one came to save me. There was no miracle this time. I knew in my heart God was there, but I couldn't feel him. Only emptiness. A darkness had overtaken me, and I felt too weak to do anything about it. My body eventually gave in to sleep and I woke early in the morning as the sun was rising, still on the floor of the family room. I couldn't do this anymore. I was going to make myself run. It was cold outside, so I dressed in a jacket, leggings, beanie, and mittens.

Running down the street and around the hill, I played the angry portion of my personal soundtrack. There were different songs that accompanied different moods, and right now it was ugly. The anger motivated me though, and I ran through the slight pain in my shins—they hadn't completely healed. I was probably two miles into my run when I crossed a section of sidewalk scarred with tire marks. The marks led to a block wall which had been patched last year. I knew what had caused this and I stopped immediately. I wanted to ignore the calming of my anger and keep it with me, but it was hard to fight against this message I was being sent.

Last year I had woken late for a run. I'd neglected to set my alarm or just plain slept through it. I'd been frustrated because it had put me behind schedule, and I only had so much time. That day as I'd run around this same hill and approached this patch of the sidewalk, there was a Jeep that had crossed oncoming traffic and jumped the curb, plowing into the block wall. The smoking Jeep had come to rest right where I should have been running a few minutes before had I woken up on time. As soon as I saw that Jeep, I knew that I had been delayed purposefully, that a divine hand had kept me from being in the path of that accident.

Seeing this landmark allowed a sliver of light to pierce the darkness that surrounded me. I remembered God's love for me, and as I made room for this the anger started to dissolve. I turned around and started to walk home. My angry motivation was gone.

I pondered my feelings as I walked. The confusion was still there. The fear as well. I had so many questions and wanted to know right now the outcome of my relationship with Drew. If only I could peer in a crystal ball and see myself in a year or two. Should I pursue the course with him or withdraw? How was this going to impact me and my kids? How would it impact him and his?

I remembered when Ezra and I were going to counseling. I didn't know our future and I felt like I was in limbo—not in one place or another. It was somewhat like that now. In between lives and not sure which to embrace. I wanted all the answers, but there was no way to have them. Then after Ezra had moved out, peace had eventually come, and I knew everything would be okay. There was part of that feeling that was trying to work its way into my heart right now. But how could I be sure of anything?

When I arrived home, I got in the shower and cranked up the hot water. I had a CPR class today as I was required to stay certified as a student and to get licensed in the next few months. Drew was coming up later today and I hoped that my mood would continue to get better. I hadn't seen him in person since all this had started and I hadn't even told him about Ezra and Amber. Drew arrived maybe a half hour after I got home from CPR. I was having a hard time keeping eye contact and knew that he had noticed.

"Mel, what's going on?" He put his hand on my arm and tried to get me to look at him.

"I don't want to cry. I know if I look at you, I'll cry," I said and immediately the tears came.

"What's wrong, Melissa? Sit down, talk to me." He gently directed me over to the couch and pulled me into him.

"I don't know. I really don't. Something has been going on with me and I have been struggling to fight it." My tears hadn't given way to sobs yet, but I was struggling to speak clearly.

Drew pulled back and looked in my eyes again. "Melissa, I love you. Talk to me, please."

"Give me a second." I stood up and grabbed a tissue from the other room. I wiped my eyes and nose and came back to the couch. "I don't know why it's affecting me so much, but I found out on Sunday that Ezra and Amber are getting divorced."

"What?!" Drew was genuinely surprised. "Has it even been a year?"

"No." I shook my head.

"That *is* surprising," he was still processing it, "but why does that have you so upset?"

"I don't know. That's what I'm trying to figure out. I've just felt so overwhelmed this week and I'm really confused and scared about the future. What if things don't work out for us, Drew? What if we get our kids all emotionally invested, and we get married and then we don't make it? I can't do that to them. I don't think I can handle it either." I looked back down at the tissue in my hands. "The way I hurt after Ezra—I think it would be worse this time if I lost you. I don't want to lose you."

"Mel…" He held my shoulders and forced me to look at him. "You're not losing me, I'm not going anywhere. Why would you even think that?"

"I didn't say you were, but what if something happens?" I questioned.

"What would happen?"

"Like what if I can't move my kids? What if your kids hate me living with them? What if we can't manage them all together and it gets to be too much?" I had more in me but quit.

"Melissa, that's why we've been taking it slow with the kids. Not pushing them. I don't have all the answers, but I don't want to lose you either. Look, it's not just *you* anymore—it's *us*. We're in this together." He pulled me back in, so my head was resting on his chest. "We're not doing anything major right away. Our kids have to finish school. *You* have to finish school. We have time to think about all of this. We'll find the answers, okay?"

His breathing was calming me down. Just being with him all the questions sounded ridiculous even to my ears and I didn't want this feeling to end. Before he left for home that night, Drew took Jake's stuffed shark that was sitting by the front door and said that he had an idea. He took it downstairs and set it on top of Jake's ceiling fan.

"He'll have fun finding that," he said. He kissed me and told me he loved me before going out to his car.

I was feeling calm and hoped it would last. The next day the kids returned in the evening and Jake went downstairs to get on his pajamas. Minutes later he came running up to me.

"Mom, was Drew here?" he asked excitedly.

"Yes, why?" I played dumb.

"When I turned on my lights, I saw my shark on the top of the fan! I had to turn the fan on to get him down. Did Drew put it up there? That was so funny!"

"Yep, he did."

This had been quite the hit. Well played, Drew. Then Jake did something that made me feel even better. He wrapped his arms around the shark and squeezed it in a tight hug.

CHAPTER 18
Circling Coyotes

The rest of February was more of the same. There was the grind of school and life, and I was getting sick of winter. Even here where it was warmer and we didn't have to deal with snow, I was tired of the cooler temperatures and wanting things to blossom and come back to life. My parents visited and I gave them a tour of my clinic. It meant a lot to me to show my dad my workspace after being his dental assistant for years. I was excited to be advancing from assistant to clinician. The written board score arrived, and I had passed! One down, two more to go. I did a small triathlon with friends and Drew met us afterward for dinner. Everyone liked him.

Austin was preparing to leave for his mission in Georgia and Drew had his brother Jackson take family photos. They turned out great, he had such a cute family. Then there was a big farewell party for Austin, and everyone gathered at a community center. Drew's ex-wife Andrea had arranged everything and had only asked for Drew to bring drinks.

I felt out of place when we arrived. Luckily Drew's parents and siblings were there, so I knew some people. But Andrea's family was there also and a lot of local friends that I didn't know. I had never met Andrea before, and today didn't end the streak. We didn't talk and there was no introduction. It wasn't like Drew and Ezra; I think we were both awkward around each other.

Austin took pictures with his friends, grandparents, and all his cousins. He didn't seem to be bothered by his parents' situation. As the party started to break up, Drew and his brothers helped put up the chairs and tables and the kids played basketball. Eventually Drew and I left, his kids would stay with their mom. Drew seemed content with how everything had gone.

But something about that awkwardness around Andrea was still sitting with me. I hated feeling out of place in this part of Drew's life and didn't know how that would change. She would always be around. Ezra would always be around. We were divorced, but we could never be rid of them because of our kids. It was so messy, all of it. I could control my little sphere with my kids, but this? How could I introduce this whole new world of stepdad and stepsiblings, Drew's parents and siblings, and new community—and would they be okay with it? If it were only me, I would run away in a heartbeat and join Drew's life, but it was different with my children that I was so protective over.

I was trying to keep all these worries to myself. I didn't want Drew to think I was questioning our relationship. It wasn't us; it was our kids and our locations. It was blending a family. How would his girls accept me as a stepmom? And how would our kids react to doing things differently? Over the next couple of weeks, I was aware of the worries building up to a simmer. By the time I saw Drew next I couldn't keep it to myself anymore.

"I'm not feeling like I was before, but I still have a lot of concerns. I'm not good at pretending everything is okay. I wish I could," I admitted to him.

"Mel don't ever pretend with me. I *want* you to tell me how you're feeling. Of course you have concerns. So do I."

"You do?" I hadn't heard this before.

"Naturally. Probably all the same things you're worried about.

I'm just trying to be patient because I think everything will sort itself out in time."

"But how do you know that?" I insisted.

"I don't. All I know is that I love you." He touched my hand. "Is that enough?"

"We're going to have to take this one day at a time," he continued. "Think how far we've come already."

I knew he was right. I couldn't expect everything to happen in a day, but it was difficult to be patient.

"We've been in some stressful situations lately. Let's do something fun. I want to take you somewhere for my birthday," he proposed. "You're on spring break then, right?"

"Right," I confirmed.

"And your kids are with their dad. So, I'm going to plan something fun, and it will be a surprise. Just a day for you to relax and not worry, okay?"

This was sounding pretty good.

"I'll get you more details later, keep that entire twenty-four hours free."

"Wow, twenty-four hours! What exactly are you planning?" I wondered aloud.

"I don't know yet, but I'm sure you'll like it. No stress, just us," he promised.

"Sounds wonderful. So, you're giving me this for *your* birthday?" I laughed.

"I can't think of anything I'd rather do for my birthday than spend the day with you." He pulled me in and kissed me, sending all my worries away.

March finally arrived, and with it some warmer temperatures. Because of spring break, my kids would be gone from me for three weekends in a row, with only a few days at home in between. The first weekend Drew and I planned a campout with his girls, and the next weekend was his birthday.

I had a nice tent that we packed, and Drew drove us down some sketchy roads in his truck to get to the campsite. The reason the roads were so concerning was that over time flooding and use had worn them down, and if you made one wrong move you could go over the edge and wind up in a wash thirty feet below. The girls and I were all gripping whatever was closest to us as we bounced over the roads. A couple of squeals may have escaped our lips. Drew was completely relaxed, and he was a good driver, so we made it there safely. As we unpacked the tent, we quickly realized something was wrong.

"Where are the poles?" Drew asked me.

"Aren't they in the bag?

"Nope. I don't think they're here." He shrugged.

"Oh no, I've only set this tent up once or twice before ever. And honestly Ezra did most of it. I thought the poles were in that bag—it's so heavy!" Panic was setting in. Had I just ruined the trip?

"No problem," Drew answered easily. "We still have a tarp, and it's great weather. We'll sleep under the stars."

"Really, is that safe? What about scorpions or animals?" I wasn't sure about this.

"I've slept outside before like this, it's fine!" Claire chimed in.

"Okay, if you guys are good with it, I am."

It was settled. We spread out the tarp and set our sleeping bags, pillows, and backpacks on it. We would go explore a bit before the sun set, then we would build a fire for dinner. There was a cave maybe two hundred feet from where we had laid our tarp and we walked that direction. There were two entrances but the upper one was closed, possibly due to unsafe conditions. As we entered from the lower access, it became dark quickly. I didn't have my flashlight on me, but my phone had one. I shined it around the rock walls, reading the inscriptions that had been there for years according to the dates accompanying the names.

Walking back out into the sunlight we decided to get the fire ready now before it got dark. We had assembled gourmet foil dinners back at Drew's place and were excited to try them out.

Typically, a foil dinner would have ground hamburger with some potatoes and carrots. But we had branched out and had done steak with mushrooms, sausage with peppers, and chicken with veggies. There was something about the sound of a sizzling foil dinner that took me right back to my childhood and here we were creating these memories with Drew's girls. After dinner we pulled out the roasting sticks and toasted marshmallows for s'mores. We unrolled our sleeping bags with Drew and I on the ends and the girls in the middle. As the fire died down, Ivy quietly brought up something I had been thinking about.

"Um, I need to go to the bathroom." She looked at me and not Drew.

"Yeah, so do I. Should we girls go find somewhere?" I asked.

"Yes," Ivy and Claire said simultaneously.

I grabbed my flashlight and we walked away from the campfire and down a path. I had stuffed some tissues in my jacket pocket and gave one to each of the girls. Strategy was discussed, as it wasn't exactly easy for girls to do this. We each found our own spot apart, but near each other. We tossed our tissues in the fire when we got back successfully and snuggled into our sleeping bags. We chatted a little as we got comfortable, then fell asleep under the stars.

In the middle of the night, I had a dream of a coyote circling our tarp and checking us out, coming near enough to sniff our scent. It startled me right out of my dream, and I sat straight up in my sleeping bag. I woke enough to see that nothing was wrong and laid back down realizing it was just a dream, falling asleep quickly.

But the next morning I discovered something that convinced me my dream had been reality. Crossing over the top of our tire tracks in the sand were the clear paw prints of a coyote. It should have scared me that this had been real, but somehow what seemed more real was the feeling of darkness that had been circling me this past month. I was doing my best to keep it at bay. It was like

I was at the precipice of something big and an unseen force was trying to hold me back.

We had brought donuts and milk for breakfast, but the girls talked us into popping the Jiffy Pop over the fire since we hadn't gotten to it the night before. So, we had donuts, milk, *and* popcorn for breakfast. We rolled up our sleeping bags, folded the tarp, and made sure the fire was extinguished before leaving the campsite. It had been a successful campout and thank goodness forgetting the tent poles hadn't resulted in us being attacked by coyotes.

With part of my spring break, I spent a morning shadowing my personal dental hygienist to fulfill a requirement for school. It was helpful to watch her natural process through each patient and exciting knowing I was only months away from being in her position. I made a casserole and brought it down to Drew's one night and we went to CrossFit together. Each day I did a ride, run, or swim in the warmth of the day since I didn't have to go in the early morning. I had lunch with several different friends, and even with Vicki and Drew's sister Hannah who was visiting. As the end of the week approached, I started to harass Drew a bit about our upcoming adventure on his birthday.

> So, what are we doing on Saturday? What should I bring with me? I need to know what to wear!

> I'm not telling you that! Just wear something comfortable.

> Should I plan on lots of walking? Do I need a change of clothes?

We will probably do some walking.
We will also use other transportation.
You shouldn't need extra clothes,
maybe a jacket though.

What kind of transportation,
are we going far?

You'll have to wait and see. There
are all kinds of transportation...

So, he was going to keep me guessing. All I really knew was to wear comfortable clothes and that we were going *somewhere*. He was picking me up super early, even for me. He had told me to be ready at 4:30 in the morning. Friday night I laid out some jeans, a t-shirt, good walking shoes, and a jacket and packed my cross-body travel purse. I showered and straightened my hair and set my alarm for four a.m.

CHAPTER 19
A Prayer and a Wish

I was ready and watching for Drew as he pulled in the driveway the next morning. We had spent all day together many times, but knowing he had something special planned and being in the dark about it had gotten me so excited. Luckily, I had fallen asleep easily the night before. It was like the night before Christmas. As he walked up the sidewalk, I opened the front door. We hugged and kissed, then I stepped back so he could see what I was wearing.

"Will this be okay today?" I asked him.

"Perfect. And you have a jacket, too. That's a good idea."

I locked the front door, and he opened his car door for me, smiling as he watched me get into the car. He was enjoying his secret to the last second. I wondered when I would figure out what we were doing. We drove in near silence. It was early and we might be driving a while I thought. But when I put it together that we were headed toward the airport, I couldn't contain myself anymore.

"We're flying somewhere! What? Where are we going?" I pelted him with questions.

He laughed. "You'll see, I'll have to give you your ticket eventually."

But he waited until the last second when we were headed through security and I needed to show it with my ID.

"Okay, here you go." He handed it to me.

I quickly scanned the ticket to find the destination city—San Francisco.

"I've never been there before!"

"I know, I listen sometimes." He smirked.

It was fortunate that it was early and uncrowded because I was probably creating a scene. We made our way through security and down the corridor to our gate. I hadn't been on a plane in several years and being here felt like an adventure already, let alone the actual destination.

"Do you have our day all planned out? I have no idea where we would even go, except maybe the Golden Gate Bridge or Chinatown or something." I was full of excited energy.

"I've got some ideas, but you get to have a day with me and *my* style of vacation planning."

He knew me too well. I would have prepared an itinerary down to the minute. Part of me wanted to do that now. But it was Drew's plan and not knowing was actually freeing. I didn't have to worry about it at all, he was in control. The flight wasn't long, but long enough that my heart calmed down and wasn't racing as much. Drew led me from the airplane to the ground transportation where we took a train into the city.

"Where are we going first?" I was curious but not pushing anymore. Just enjoying the ride.

"How about Chinatown?" He didn't seem to be in any rush.

We used our phones and the city maps to help us determine which train line to take. The yellow line took us to Powell Street Station, not far from Union Square. We walked past store after store, stepping in a few to look around. There was an art exhibit on the main square, and we took pictures of and with some of the pieces. We kept heading north toward Chinatown, and I could tell when we were getting close. Soon there were less English signs and many more in Chinese or with Chinese characters next to the English words. The hustle and bustle in Chinatown was different from the rest of the city. Businesses were closer together and there appeared to be as much to look at out on the sidewalk as inside the shops.

Eventually we were ready for lunch and found a Chinese restaurant to try. The food was good, but I'd had a hard time ordering. It was apparently more authentic than anywhere I had been before. As we ate, we discussed what we would do with the rest of the day.

"I was thinking we could go to the San Francisco Botanical Garden, if that's okay with you," Drew checked with me.

"That sounds great! I've never been anywhere here, so it is all new to me!"

"Then after that we can come back this way, but north a bit to Little Italy. You'd love to have dinner there, I'm sure." He knew he was right.

"Of course, I'd never turn down Italian."

"And Little Italy isn't far from Fisherman's Wharf, where can get a good view of Golden Gate Bridge," he continued.

"Those are two places I've heard of, so I'd love to see them! By the way, how's your birthday going?" I had wished him a happy birthday first thing this morning but didn't want to forget this was *his* day, not mine.

"This has to be one of the best birthdays ever, and I hope it's only going to get better," he told me.

He paid for lunch, and we walked back out onto the busy sidewalk. We consulted our phones again and discovered the easiest route. We took a bus back down to Powell Station, saving on the walking time and then the red light rail track took us west to the Botanical Garden. At the entrance we checked out the large map and got a brochure version to carry with us. The gardens were huge with so much to see and were only a portion of Golden Gate Park. The park was also home to several museums and recreational fields with an incredible trail system winding throughout.

The names of the garden paths gave a hint toward what type of flora and fauna you might encounter. There was the "Australia

Walk," the "Dwarf Conifer Path," and the "Redwood Walk." Gardens had names like "Temperate Asia," "Garden of Fragrance," and one of my favorites was "Succulent Garden." I had been sure to bring my nicer camera in my purse. It was a simple point and shoot, but better than my phone's camera. Everything was so beautiful. It was hard to not take pictures at each turn.

We had been walking for quite some time, and Drew spotted a wooden bench removed from the main path. It had a wooden structure surrounding it with a trellis overtop. We sat down, but Drew didn't stay for long. He grabbed something out of his jacket pocket and got down in front of me on one knee. My heart started thumping, I could only think of one reason why he would be doing this.

"Melissa, I can't wait any longer." He presented a small box and opened it, revealing a diamond ring. "I have been worried about losing this all day!" he laughed. "You have to know how I feel about you. You are an amazing woman and have brought so much happiness into my life. I want you with me every day. Every night. Always. There are a lot of things we need to figure out, but I want you to know that you can't scare me away. Your kids can't scare me away. I need you, and your problems are mine now. I want to be there with you to make you laugh, to hold you when you cry. I will work the rest of my life to be the man you deserve. Melissa, will you marry me?"

I burst out in tears. I could think of nothing I wanted more than to be with him every day.

"Yes, Drew. Yes!" I held out my hand, helping him slide the ring onto my finger.

He half stood to reach my lips with his and we kissed through my tears and his. We took several pictures, selfies of us on "our" bench and of Drew holding my hand with its new ornamentation. The ring was a beautifully clear princess cut diamond, uniquely set on point on a thin white gold band that fit my slim finger perfectly.

I took many more pictures that day of my hand everywhere we went. I was walking on clouds.

After making our way through the gardens, we found how to get transportation to Fisherman's Wharf. Tied up along the pier were tour boats to get better views of the Golden Gate Bridge and Alcatraz.

"We've got a while before dinner. What do you think?" Drew pointed at a boat we had passed.

"I would love that!"

Being on the water would make this day complete. We walked over and boarded the boat just in time. As we neared the famous landmark, the captain announced that it was tradition to make a wish under the Golden Gate Bridge. I readied my camera and snapped a selfie as the boat stopped for a moment underneath. Then I put my camera away and held Drew's hand, closing my eyes as I made my wish in secret.

Thank you. I said a prayer in my heart as a prelude to my wish. *I never dreamed I could be this happy. But I need to ask for more. Please help us to make this work. Please guide us as we try to do what is best not only for us but our children as well. Thank you for putting Drew in my life, and my wish is that he and I will be able to create our happily ever after with your help.*

I opened my eyes and saw that Drew had been watching me. I wondered what he had wished, surely something similar. As he leaned in and kissed me, I knew that we hadn't found each other by chance. I knew that we were each other's blessing. Even if our future wasn't easy, our happiness was tied together and knowing that gave me the courage to face any trials that were ahead. By his side, we could do anything together and I couldn't wait to spend each day with him.

END

EPILOGUE

Something was missing. I wasn't unhappy; I really enjoyed my life with Drew, but it was like I had lost my purpose. When we'd met, I had been driven by triathlon, school, and basic survival with the kids. After we married, I had tapered off triathlon, doing CrossFit with Drew and pouring my time into our family and work.

Now with this new move and most of our kids graduated, we had become empty nesters overnight and I seemed a little off-track. In the 6 years we had been married I had gained more weight than I wanted to admit. Not exactly the peak condition I was in before. I couldn't blame it on age as I was now 42, the same age Drew had been when we met. The hour-long commute to work both ways had absorbed a lot of time, and so had our family. But now I had none of those excuses. What was I waiting for and what did I need to move forward? I needed a new goal, new purpose.

Then one day at work I met someone, a young woman who was about to embark on a three-day train ride to Maine with her father. Their plan was to use this trip to write. Something stirred in me that I had never felt before. I asked her more about her writing, and she mentioned that it was always good to write about something you had some knowledge of or experience with.

I so often spoke with patients and even strangers about my experience with divorce, remarriage, and blending a family and had come to realize how many were affected by these same situations.

Dental cleanings turned into therapy sessions for my patients (and myself), and I wished I could share more of my experience and message. Maybe I could. I would write my story.

Stay tuned for the sequel to *Strength on the Water.*

Printed in the United States
by Baker & Taylor Publisher Services